ST. THOMAS AQUINAS

ON PRAYER AND THE CONTEMPLATIVE LIFE

ST. THOMAS AQUINAS

ON PRAYER AND THE CONTEMPLATIVE LIFE

# ON PRAYER
## AND THE
# CONTEMPLATIVE LIFE

BY ST. THOMAS AQUINAS

# CONTENTS

QUESTION LXXXI

OF THE VIRTUE OF RELIGION

I

Does the Virtue of Religion direct a Man to God Alone?

Cicero says: "Religion offers internal and external reverence to that Superior Nature which we term the Divine."

S. Isidore says: "A religious man is, as Cicero remarks, so called from *religion*, for he is occupied with and, as it were, reads through again and again (*relegit*) the things that concern Divine worship." Thus religion seems to be so called from reading again (*religendo*) things concerning Divine worship; for such things are to be repeatedly revolved in the mind, according to those words of Proverbs iii. 6: *In all thy ways think on Him.* At the same time *religion* might be said to be so called because "we ought to choose again (*re-eligere*) those things which through our negligence we have lost," as S. Augustine has noted. Or perhaps it is better derived from "binding again" (*religando*); thus S. Augustine says: "Let religion bind us once more to the One Almighty God."

But whether religion be so called from frequent *reading*, or from *fresh election* of Him Whom we have negligently lost, or from *rebinding*, it properly implies a certain relation to God. For it is He to Whom we ought to be especially *bound* as our indefectible principle; to Him must we assiduously direct our *choice* as our ultimate end; He it is Whom we negligently lose by sin and Whom we must regain by believing in Him and by professing our faith in Him.

But some deny that religion directs a man to God alone, thus:

1. S. James says: *Religion clean and undefiled before God and the Father is this: to visit the fatherless and widows in their tribulation; and to keep oneself unspotted from this world.* But *to visit the fatherless and widows* indicates relation to our neighbour, and *to keep oneself unspotted from this world* refers to ourselves. Hence religion is not confined to our relationship with God.

But religion has two sorts of acts. Some belong to it properly and immediately, those acts, namely, which it elicits and by which man is directed to God alone, as, for instance, to offer Him sacrifice, to adore Him, etc.

But there are other acts which religion produces through the medium of the virtues which it controls, directing them, that is, towards reverence to God; for that virtue which is concerned with the end directs those virtues which have to do with the means to the end. And in this sense *to visit the fatherless and widows in their tribulation* is said to be an act of religion because commanded by it, though actually elicited by the virtue of mercy. Similarly *to keep oneself unspotted from this world* is an act commanded by religion, though elicited by temperance or some other virtue.

2. S. Augustine says: "Since according to the genius of the Latin speech—and that not merely of the unlearned, but even of the most learned—religion is said to be shown towards our human relatives and connexions and intimates, this word 'religion' cannot be used without some ambiguity when applied to the worship of God; hence we cannot say with absolute confidence that religion is nought else but the worship of God." Religion, then, is not limited to our relation to God, but embraces, our neighbour as well.

But it is only by an extension of the name "religion" that it is made to embrace our relations towards our human kin, it is not according to the proper signification of the word. Hence S. Augustine prefaced the words quoted from him above with the remark: "Religion, strictly speaking, seems to mean, not any kind of worship, but only that of God."

3. Further, *latria* seems to come under religion. But S. Augustine says: "*Latria* is interpreted as service." But we ought to serve not God only, but our neighbour as well: *By charity of the spirit serve one another.* Religion, then, implies relation to our neighbour.

But since a slave implies a master, it follows that where there exists a peculiar and special title of dominion there also will be found a peculiar and special ratio of servitude. It is clear, however, that dominion belongs to God in a peculiar and special fashion, since He it is Who has made all things and Who holds the chief rule over all things. Consequently a special kind of service is due to Him. And this service is by the Greeks designated *latria*, which is, in consequence, properly comprised under "religion."

4. Again, reverence comes under religion. But man has to reverence, not only God, but his neighbour as well; as Cato says: "Reverence parents." Hence religion establishes a relation between ourselves and our neighbour as well as between ourselves and God.

But we are said to reverence those men whom we honour or remember, or to whose presence we resort. So, too, even things which are subject to us are said to be "cultivated" by us (*coli*); thus husbandmen (*agricolæ*) are so called because they "cultivate" the fields; the inhabitants of a place, too (*incolæ*), are so called because they "cultivate" the spots where they dwell. But since special honour is due to God as the First Principle of all, a special kind of "cultus" or "reverence" is His due, and this the Greeks call *eusebia* or *theosebia*, as S. Augustine says.

5. Lastly, all who are in a state of salvation are subject to God. But not all who are in a state of salvation are called "religious," but those only who bind themselves by certain vows and observances and who undertake to obey certain men. Hence religion does not seem to mean the relationship of subjection of man to God.

But although, generally speaking, all those who worship God can be termed "religious," yet those are specially so called who dedicate their whole lives to the Divine worship and cut themselves off from worldly occupations.

Thus those are not termed "contemplatives" who merely contemplate, but they who devote their lives to contemplation. And such men do not subject themselves to men for man's sake, but for God's, as the Apostle says: *You received me as an Angel of God, even as Christ Jesus.*

*S. Augustine*: We are to abide in Christ! How then shall That not be now our possession Where we are then to abide and Whence we are to draw Life? Let Holy Scripture speak for us lest we should seem in mere conjecture to be saying things contrary to the teaching of the Word of God. Hear the words of one who knew: *If God be for us who is against us? The Lord,* he says, *is the portion of my inheritance.* He saith not: Lord, what wilt Thou give me for mine inheritance? All that Thou canst give me is worthless! Be Thou mine inheritance! Thee do I love! Thee do I wholly love! With all my heart, with all my soul, with all my mind do I love Thee! What, then, shall be my lot? What wilt Thou give me save Thyself? This is to love God freely. This is to hope for God from God. This is to hasten to be filled with God, to be sated with Him. For He is sufficient for thee; apart from Him nought can suffice thee! (*Sermon,* cccxxxiv. 3).

*S. Augustine*: I cried to the Lord with my voice. Many cry to the Lord that they may win riches, that they may avoid losses; they cry that their family may be established, they ask for temporal happiness, for worldly dignities; and, lastly, they cry for bodily health, which is the patrimony of the poor. For these and suchlike things many cry to the Lord; hardly one cries for the Lord Himself! How easy it is for a man to desire all manner of things from the Lord and yet not desire the Lord Himself! As though the gift could be sweeter than the Giver! (*on Ps.* lxxvi.).

*S. Augustine:* Picture God as saying to you—He Who re-created you and adopted you: "My son, why is it that day by day you rise and pray, and genuflect, and even strike the ground with your forehead, nay, sometimes even shed tears, while you say to Me: 'My Father, my God! give me wealth!' If I were to give it to you, you would think yourself of some importance, you would fancy you had gained something very great. Yet because you asked for it you have it. But take care to make good use of it. Before you had it you were humble; now that you have begun to be rich you despise the poor! What kind of a good is that which only makes you worse? For worse you are, since you were bad already. And that it would make you worse you knew not, hence you asked it of Me. I gave it to you and I proved you; you have found—and you are found out! You were hidden when you had nothing. Correct thyself! Vomit up this cupidity! Take a draught of charity!... Ask of Me better things than these, greater things than these. Ask of Me spiritual things. Ask of Me Myself!" (*Sermon,* cccxi. 14-15).

## II

Is Religion a Virtue?

A virtue is that which both renders its possessor, as also his work, good. Hence we must say that every good act comes under virtue. And it is clear that to render to another what is his due has the character of a good act; for by the fact that a man renders to another his due there is established a certain fitting proportion and order between them. But order comes under the ratio of good, just as do measure and species, as S. Augustine establishes. Since, then, it belongs to religion to render to some one, namely, God, the honour which is His due, it is clear that religion is a virtue.

Some, however, deny this, thus:

1. It belongs to religion to show reverence to God. But reverence is an act of fear, and fear is a gift. Religion, then, is a gift, not a virtue.

To reverence God is indeed an act of the gift of fear. But to religion it belongs to do certain things by reason of our reverence for God. Hence it does not follow that religion is the same thing as the gift of fear, but it is related to it as to a higher principle. For the gifts are superior to the moral virtues.

2. All virtue consists in the free-will, and hence virtue is called an elective or voluntary habit. But *latria* belongs to religion, and *latria* implies a certain servitude. Hence religion is not a virtue.

But even a servant can freely give to his master the service that is his due and thus "make a virtue of necessity" by voluntarily paying his debt. And similarly the payment of due service to God can be an act of virtue according as a man does it voluntarily.

3. Lastly, as is said in Aristotle's *Ethics*, the aptitude for the virtues is implanted in us by nature; hence those things which come under the virtues arise from the dictates of natural reason; but it belongs to religion to offer external reverence to the Divine Nature. Ceremonial, however, or external reverence, is not due to the dictates of natural reason. Hence religion is not a virtue. But it is due to the dictates of natural reason that a man does certain things in order to show reverence to God. That he should do precisely this or that, however, does not come from the dictates of natural reason, but from Divine or human positive law.

## III

Is Religion One Virtue?

S. Paul says to the Ephesians: *One God, one faith.* But true religion maintains faith in one God. Consequently religion is one virtue.

Habits are distinguished according to the divers objects with which they are concerned. But it belongs to religion to show reverence for the One God for one particular reason, inasmuch, namely, as He is the First Principle, the Creator and Governor of all things; hence we read in Malachi: *If I am a Father, where is my honour?* for it is the father that produces and governs. Hence it is clear that religion is but one virtue.

But some maintain that religion is not one virtue, thus:

1. By religion we are ordained to God. But in God there are Three Persons, and, moreover, divers attributes which are at least distinguishable from one another by reason. But the diverse character of the objects on which they fall suffices to differentiate the virtues. Hence religion is not one virtue.

But the Three Divine Persons are but One Principle as concerns the creation and the government of things. And consequently They are to be served by one religion. And the divers attributes all concur in the First Principle, for God produces all and governs all by His Wisdom, His Will, and the power of His Goodness. Hence religion is but one virtue.

2. One virtue can have but one act; for habits are differentiated according to their acts. But religion has many acts, *e.g.*, to worship, to serve, to make vows, to pray, to make sacrifices, and many other similar things. Consequently religion is not one virtue.

But by one and the same act does man serve God and worship Him; for worship is referred to God's excellence, to which is due reverence: service regards man's subjection, for by reason of his condition he is bound to show reverence to God. And under these two heads are comprised all the acts which are attributed to religion; for by them all man makes protestation of the Divine excellence and of his subjection of himself to God, either by offering Him something, or, again, by taking upon himself something Divine.

3. Further, adoration belongs to religion. But adoration is paid to images for one reason and to God for another. But since diversity of "reason" serves to differentiate the virtues, it seems that religion is not one virtue. But religious worship is not paid to images considered in themselves as entities, but precisely as images bringing God Incarnate to our mind. Further, regarding an image precisely as an image of some one, we do not stop at it; it carries us on to that which it represents. Hence the fact that religious veneration is paid to images of Christ in no sense means that there are various kinds of *latria*, nor different virtues of religion.

IV

Is Religion a Special Virtue Distinct From Others?

Religion is regarded as a part of Justice, and is distinct from the other parts of Justice.

Since virtue is ordained to what is good, where there exists some special ratio of good there must be some special corresponding virtue. But the particular good towards which religion is ordained is the showing due honour to God. Honour, however, is due by reason of some excellency. And to God belongs pre-eminent excellence, since He in every possible way infinitely transcends all things. Hence special honour is due to Him; just as we note that in human concerns varying honours are due to the varying excellencies of persons; one is the honour of a father, another that of a king, and so on. Hence it is manifest that religion is a special virtue.

Some, however, maintain that religion is not a special virtue distinct from others, thus:

1. S. Augustine says: "True sacrifice is every work undertaken in order that we may be joined to God in holy fellowship." But sacrifice comes under religion. Every work of virtue therefore comes under religion. And consequently it is not a special virtue.

But every work of virtue is said to be a sacrifice in so far as it is directed to showing God reverence. It does not thence follow that religion is a general virtue, but that it commands all the other virtues.

2. The Apostle says to the Corinthians: *Do all to the glory of God.* But it belongs to religion to do some things for the glory of God. Hence religion is not a special virtue.

But all kinds of acts, in so far as they are done for the glory of God, come under religion; not, however, as though it elicited them, but inasmuch as it controls them. Those acts, however, come under religion as eliciting them which, by their own specific character, pertain to the service of God.

3. Lastly, the charity whereby we love God is not distinct from the charity by which we love our neighbour. But in the *Ethics* it is said: "To be honoured is akin to being loved." Hence religion by which God is honoured is not a specifically distinct virtue from those observances, whether *dulia* or piety, whereby we honour our neighbour. Hence it is not a special virtue.

But the object of love is a *good* thing; whereas the object of honour or reverence is what is *excellent.* But it is God's Goodness that is communicated to His creatures, not the excellence of His Goodness. Hence while the charity wherewith we love God is not a distinct virtue from the charity wherewith we love our neighbour, yet the religion whereby we honour God is distinct from the virtues whereby we honour our neighbour.

V

Is Religion One of the Theological Virtues?

Religion is considered a part of Justice, and this is a moral virtue.

Religion is the virtue whereby we offer to God His due honour. Two things have therefore to be considered in religion. First we have to consider what religion offers God, namely, worship: this may be regarded as the material and the object with which religion is concerned.

Secondly, we have to consider Him to Whom it is offered, namely, God Himself. Now, when worship is offered to God it is not as though our worshipful acts touched God, though this is the case when we believe God, for by believing in God we touch Him (and we have therefore said elsewhere that God is the object of our faith not simply inasmuch as we believe in God, but inasmuch as we believe God). Due worship, however, is offered to God in that certain acts whereby we worship Him are performed as homage to Him, the offering sacrifice, for instance, and so forth. From all which it is evident that God does not stand to the virtue of religion as its object or as the material with which it is concerned, but as its goal. And consequently religion is not a theological virtue, for the object of these latter is the ultimate end; but religion is a moral virtue, and the moral virtues are concerned with the means to the end.

But some regard religion as a theological virtue, thus:

1. S. Augustine says: "God is worshipped by faith, hope, and charity," and these are theological virtues. But to offer worship to God comes under religion. Therefore religion is a theological virtue.

But it is always the case that a faculty or a virtue whose object is a certain end, controls—by commanding—those faculties or virtues which have to do with those things which are means to that end. But the theological virtues—*i.e.*, faith, hope, and charity—are directly concerned with God as their proper object. And hence they are the cause—by commanding it—of the act of the virtue of religion which does certain things having relation to God. It is in this sense that S. Augustine says that "God is worshipped by faith, hope, and charity."

2. Those are called theological virtues which have God for their object. But religion has God for its object, for it directs us to God alone. Therefore it is a theological virtue.

But religion directs man to God, not indeed as towards its object, but as towards its goal.

3. Lastly, every virtue is either theological or intellectual or moral. But religion is not an intellectual virtue, for its perfection does not consist in the consideration of the truth. Neither is it a moral virtue, for the property of the moral virtues is to steer a middle course betwixt what is superfluous and what is below the requisite; whereas no one can worship God to excess, according to the words of Ecclesiasticus: *For He is above all praise.* Religion, then, can only be a theological virtue.

But religion is neither an intellectual nor a theological virtue, but a moral virtue, for it is part of justice. And the *via media* in religion lies, not between the passions, but in a certain harmony which it establishes in the acts which are directed towards God. I say "a certain," not an absolute harmony, for we can never show to God all the worship that is His due; I mean, then, the harmony arising from the consideration of our human powers and of the Divine acceptance of what we offer. Moreover, there can be excess in those things which have to do with the Divine worship; not indeed as regards quantity, but in certain other circumstances, as, for example, when Divine worship is offered to whom it should not, or at times when it should not, or in other unfitting circumstances.

VI

Is Religion to be preferred to the Other Moral Virtues?

In Exodus the commandments which concern religion are put first, as though they were of primary importance. But the order of the commandments is proportioned to the order of the virtues; for the commandments of the Law fall upon the acts of the virtues. Hence religion is chief among the moral virtues.

The means to an end derive their goodness from their relation to that end; hence the more nigh they are to the end the better they are. But the moral virtues are concerned with those things which are ordained to God as their goal. And religion approaches more nearly to God than do the other moral virtues, inasmuch as it is occupied with those things which are directly and immediately ordained to the Divine honour. Hence religion is the chief of the moral virtues.

Some, however, deny that religion is pre-eminent among the moral virtues, thus:

1. The perfection of a moral virtue lies in this, that it keeps the due medium. But religion fails to attain the medium of justice, for it does not render to God anything absolutely equal to Him. Hence religion is not better than the other moral virtues.

But the praiseworthiness of a virtue lies in the will, not in the power. Hence to fall short of equality—which is the midpath of justice—for lack of power, does not make virtue less praiseworthy, provided the deficiency is not due to the will.

2. Again, in our service of men a thing seems to be praiseworthy in proportion to the need of him whom we assist; hence it is said in Isaias: *Deal thy bread to the hungry.* But God needs nothing that we can offer Him, according to the Psalmist: *I have said: Thou art my God, for Thou hast no need of my goods.* Hence religion seems to be less praiseworthy than the other virtues, for by them man is succoured.

But in the service we render to another for his profit, that is the more praiseworthy which is rendered to the most needy, because it is of greater profit to him. But no service is rendered to God for His profit—for His glory, indeed, but for our profit.

3. Lastly, the greater the necessity for doing a thing the less worthy it is of praise, according to the words: *For if I preach the Gospel, it is no glory to me, for a necessity lieth upon me.* But the greater the debt the greater the necessity. Since, then, the service which man offers to God is the greatest of debts, it would appear that religion is the least praiseworthy of all human virtues.

Where necessity comes in the glory of supererogation is non-existent; but the merit of the virtue is not thereby excluded, provided the will be present. Consequently the argument does not follow.

VII

Has Religion, That is *Latria*, any External Acts?

In Ps. lxxxiii. 3 it is said: *My heart and my flesh have rejoiced in the living God.* Now interior acts belong to the heart, and in the same way exterior acts are referred to the members of the body. It appears, then, that God is to be worshipped by exterior as well as by interior acts.

We do not show reverence and honour to God for His own sake—for He in Himself is filled with glory to which nought can be added by any created thing—but for our own sakes. For by the fact that we reverence and honour God our minds are subjected to Him, and in that their perfection lies; for all things are perfected according as they are subjected to that which is superior to them—the body, for instance, when vivified by the soul, the air when illumined by the sun. Now the human mind needs—if it would be united to God—the guidance of the things of sense; for, as the Apostle says to the Romans: *The invisible things of Him are clearly seen, being understood by the things that are made.* Hence in the Divine worship it is necessary to make use of certain corporal acts, so that by their means, as by certain signs, man's mind may be stirred up to those spiritual acts whereby it is knit to God. Consequently religion has certain interior acts which are its chief ones and which essentially belong to it; but it has also external acts which are secondary and which are subordinated to the interior acts.

Some deny, however, that exterior acts belong to religion or *latria*, thus:

1. In S. John iv. 24 we read: *For God is a Spirit, and they that adore Him must adore Him in spirit and in truth.* External acts belong, however, rather to the body than to the spirit. Consequently religion, which comprises adoration, has no exterior acts, but only interior.

But here the Lord speaks only of that which is chiefest and which is essentially intended in Divine worship.

2. The end of religion is to show reverence and honour to God. But it is not reverent to offer to a superexcellent person what properly belongs to inferiors. Since, then, what a man offers by bodily acts seems more in accordance with men's needs and with that respect which we owe to inferior created beings, it does not appear that it can fittingly be made use of in order to show reverence to God.

But such external acts are not offered to God as though He needed them, as He says in the Psalm: *Shall I eat the flesh of bullocks? Or shall I drink the blood of goats?* But such acts are offered to God as signs of those interior and spiritual works which God accepts for their own sakes. Hence S. Augustine says: "The visible sacrifice is the sacrament—that is, the visible sign—of the invisible sacrifice."

3. Lastly, S. Augustine praises Seneca for his condemnation of those men who offered to their idols what they were wont to offer to men: on the ground, namely, that what belongs to mortal men is not fittingly offered to the immortals. Still less, then, can such things be fittingly offered to the True God Who is *above all gods*. Therefore to worship God by means of bodily acts seems to be reprehensible. And consequently religion does not include bodily acts.

But idolaters are so called because they offer to their idols things belonging to men, and this not as outward signs which may excite in them spiritual affections, but as being acceptable by those idols for their own sake. And especially because they offered them empty and vile things.

*S. Augustine:* When men pray, they, as becomes suppliants, make use of their bodily members, for they bend the knee, they stretch forth their hands, they even prostrate on the ground and perform other visible acts. Yet all the while their invisible will and their heart's intention are known to God. He needs not these signs for the human soul to be laid bare before Him. But man by so doing stirs himself up to pray and groan with greater humility and fervour. I know not how it is that whereas such bodily movements can only be produced by reason of some preceding act on the part of the soul, yet when they are thus visibly performed the interior invisible movement which gave them birth is thereby itself increased, and the heart's affections—which must have preceded, else such acts would not have been performed—are thereby themselves increased.

Yet none the less, if a man be in some sort hindered so that he is not at liberty to make use of such external acts, the interior man does not therefore cease to pray; in the secret chamber of his heart, where lies compunction, he lies prostrate before the eyes of God (*Of Care for the Dead*, v.).

VIII

Is Religion the Same as Sanctity?

In S. Luke's Gospel we read: *Let us serve Him in holiness and justice.* But to serve God comes under religion. Hence religion is the same as sanctity.

The word "sanctity" seems to imply two things. First, it seems to imply *cleanness*, and this is in accordance with the Greek word for it, for in Greek it is *hagios*, as though meaning "without earth." Secondly, it implies *stability*, and thus among the ancients those things were termed *sancta* which were so hedged about with laws that they were safe from violation; similarly a thing is said to be *sancitum* because established by law. And even according to the Latins the word *sanctus* may mean "cleanness," as derived from *sanguine tinctus*, for of old those who were to be purified were sprinkled with the blood of a victim, as says S. Isidore in his *Etymologies*.

And both meanings allow us to attribute sanctity to things which are used in the Divine worship; so that not men only, but also temples and vessels and other similar things are said to be sanctified by reason of their use in Divine worship. *Cleanness* indeed is necessary if a man's mind is to be applied to God. For the mind of man is stained by being immersed in inferior things, as indeed all things are cheapened by admixture with things inferior to them—silver, for instance, when mixed with lead. And for our minds to be knit to the Supreme Being they must needs be withdrawn from inferior things. Without cleanness, then, the mind cannot be applied to God. Hence in the Epistle to the Hebrews it is said: *Follow peace with all men, and holiness, without which no man shall see God.*

*Stability* is also required if the mind is to be applied to God. For the mind is applied to Him as to the Ultimate End and First Principle, and consequently must be immovable. Hence the Apostle says: *For I am sure that neither death nor life shall separate me from the love of God.*

Sanctity, then, is said to be that whereby man's mind and its acts are applied to God. Hence sanctity does not differ from religion essentially, but in idea only. For by religion we mean that a man offers God due service in those things which specially pertain to the Divine worship—sacrifices, for example, and oblations, etc.; but by sanctity we mean that a man not only offers these things, but also refers to God the works of the other virtues, and also that a man disposes himself by good works for the Divine worship.

Some, however, deny the identity of religion and sanctity, thus:

1. Religion is a certain special virtue. But sanctity is called a general virtue, for according to Andronicus, sanctity is that which "makes men faithful observers of what is justly due to God." Hence sanctity is not the same as religion.

But sanctity is in its essence a special virtue, and as such is, in a sort, the same as religion. It has, however, a certain general aspect in that, by its commands, it directs all the acts of the virtues to the Divine Good. In the same way legal justice is termed a general virtue in that it directs the acts of all the virtues to the common good.

2. Sanctity seems to imply cleanness, for S. Denis says: "Sanctity is freedom from all impurity; it is perfect and stainless cleanness." Cleanness, however, seems to come under temperance, for this it is which precludes bodily defilement. Since, then, religion comes under justice, sanctity cannot be identified with religion.

Temperance indeed worketh cleanness, but this has not the ratio of sanctity except it be referred to God. Hence S. Augustine says of virginity itself that "not because it is virginity is it held in honour, but because it is consecrated to God."

3. Lastly, things that are contradistinguished are not identical. But in all enumerations of the parts of justice sanctity is set against religion.

But sanctity is set against religion because of the difference aforesaid; they differ indeed in idea, not in substance.

*Cajetan:* Religion is directly concerned with those things which specially pertain to the Divine worship—ceremonies, for example, sacrifices, oblations, etc. Whereas sanctity directly regards the mind, and through the mind the other virtuous works, including those of religion … for it makes use of them so as thereby to apply the mind—and by consequence all acts that proceed from the human mind—to God. Thus we see that many religious people are not saints, whereas all saints are religious. For people who devote themselves to ceremonies, sacrifices, etc., can be termed religious; but they can only be called saints in so far as by means of these things they give themselves interiorly to God (*on* 2. 2. 81. 8).

## QUESTION LXXXII

## OF DEVOTION

### I

### Is Devotion a Special Kind of Act?

It is by our acts that we merit. But devotion has a peculiarly meritorious character. Consequently devotion is a special kind of act.

Devotion is so termed from "devoting" oneself. Hence the "devout" are so named because they "devote" themselves to God and thus proclaim their complete subjection to Him. Thus, too, among the heathen of old those were termed "devout" who for the army's sake "devoted" themselves to their idols unto death, as Livy tells us was the case with the two Decii. Hence devotion seems to mean nothing else than "the will to give oneself promptly to those things which pertain to God's service"; thus it is said in Exodus: *The multitude of the children of Israel ... offered first-fruits to the Lord with a most ready and devout mind.* It is clear, however, that a wish to do *readily* what belongs to God's service is a special act. Hence devotion is a special act of the will.

But some argue that devotion is not a special kind of act, thus:

1. That which serves to qualify other acts cannot be itself a special act. But devotion appears to qualify certain other acts; thus it is said that *all the multitude offered victims, and praises, and holocausts with a devout mind.*

But that which moves another gives a certain measure to the latter's movement. The will, however, moves the other faculties of the soul to their respective acts; and, moreover, the will, as aiming at an end in view, moves itself to the means towards that end. Consequently, since devotion is the act of a man who offers himself to serve Him Who is the Ultimate End, it follows that devotion gives a certain measure to human acts—whether they be the acts of the will itself with regard to the means to an end, or the acts of the other faculties as moved by the will.

2. Again, no act which finds a place in different kinds of acts can be itself a special kind of act. But devotion is to be found in acts of different kinds, both in corporal acts, for example, and in spiritual; thus a man is said to meditate devoutly, for instance, or to genuflect devoutly.

But devotion does not find a place in different kinds of acts as though it were a *species* coming under different *genera*, but in the same sense as the motive power of a moving principle is virtually discoverable in the movements of the things it sets in motion.

3. Lastly, all special kinds of acts belong either to the appetitive or to the cognoscitive faculties. But devotion comes under neither of these—as will be evident to anyone who will reflect upon the various acts of these faculties respectively.

13

But devotion is an act of the appetitive powers of the soul, and is, as we have said above, a movement of the will.

*Cajetan:* With regard to the proper meaning of the term *devotion*, note that since *devotion* is clearly derived from *devoting*, and since *to devote*—derived in its turn from *to vow*—means to promise something spontaneously to God: it follows that the principle in all such promises is the will; and further, not the will simply as such, but the will so affected as to be prompt. Hence in Latin those are said to be *devoted* to some superior whose will is so affected towards him as to make them prompt in his regard. And this seems to refer especially to God and to those who in a sense stand in His place, as, for instance, our rulers, our fatherland, and our principles of action. Hence in the Church's usage the term *devotion* is especially applied to those who are so affected towards God as to be prompt in His regard and in all that concerns Him. And so *devotion* is here taken to signify the act of a will so disposed, the act by which a man shows himself prompt in the Divine service.... Thus, then, *devotion*, the principal act of the virtue of religion, implies first of all the prompt desire of the Divine honour in our exercise of Divine worship; and hence comes the prompt choice of appropriate means to this end, and also the prompt carrying out of what we see to be suitable to that end. And the proof of possession of such *devotion* is that truly devout souls, the moment they perceive that some particular thing (or other) ought to be done for the service of God, are so promptly moved towards it that they rejoice in having to do or in actually doing it (*on* 2. 2. 82. 1).

*S. Augustine:* Give me, O Lord, Thyself; grant Thyself to me! For Thee do I love, and if my love be but weak, then would I love Thee more. For I cannot measure it so as to know how much my love falls short of that love which shall make my life run to Thy embraces nor ever turn away from Thee till I be hid in the hiding-place of Thy countenance. This only do I know: that it fares ill with me when away from Thee; and this not merely externally, but within me; for all abundance which is not my God is but penury for me! (*Confessions*, XIII. viii. 2).

II

Is Devotion an Act of the Virtue of Religion?

Devotion is derived from "devoting oneself" or making vows. But a vow is an act of the virtue of religion. Consequently devotion also is an act of the virtue of religion.

It belongs to the same virtue to wish to do a thing and to have a prompt will to do it, for the object of each of these acts is the same. For this reason the Philosopher says: "Justice is that by which men will and perform just deeds." And it is clear that to perform those things which pertain to the Divine worship or service comes under the virtue of religion. Consequently it belongs to the same virtue of religion to have a prompt will to carry out these things—in other words, to be devout. Whence it follows that devotion is an act of the virtue of religion.

But some argue that devotion is not an act of the virtue of religion, thus:

1. Devotion means that a man gives himself to God. But this belongs to the virtue of charity, for, as S. Denis says: "Divine love causes ecstasy since it permits not that those who love should belong any more to themselves, but to those things which they love." Whence devotion would seem to be rather an act of charity than of the virtue of religion.

It is indeed through charity that a man gives himself to God, clinging to Him by a certain union of soul; but that a man should give himself to God and occupy himself with the Divine service, is due directly to the virtue of religion, though indirectly it is due to the virtue of charity, which is the principle of the virtue of religion.

2. Again, charity precedes the virtue of religion. But devotion seems to precede charity; for charity is signified in Scripture by fire, and devotion by the fat of the sacrifices—the material on which the fire feeds. Consequently devotion is not an act of the virtue of religion.

But while the fat of the body is generated by the natural digestive heat, that natural heat finds its nourishment in that same fat. Similarly charity both causes devotion—since it is by love that a man becomes prompt to serve his friend—and at the same time charity is fed by devotion; just as all friendship is preserved and increased by the practice of friendly acts and by meditating upon them.

3. Lastly, by the virtue of religion a man turns to God alone. But devotion extends to men as well; people, for instance, are said to be devoted to certain Saints, and servants are said to be devoted to their masters, as S. Leo says of the Jews, that being devoted to the Roman laws, they said: *We have no king but Cæsar.* Consequently devotion is not an act of the virtue of religion.

But the devotion which we have to the Saints of God, whether living or dead, does not stop at them, but passes on to God, since we venerate God in God's ministers. And the devotion which subjects have to their temporal masters is of a different kind altogether, just as the service of temporal masters differs from the service of the Divine Master.

III

Is Contemplation, that is Meditation, the Cause of Devotion?

In Ps. xxxviii. 4 it is said: *And in my meditation a fire shall flame out.* But spiritual fire causes devotion. Therefore meditation causes devotion.

The extrinsic and principal cause of devotion is God Himself; thus S. Ambrose says: "God calls those whom He deigns to call; and whom He wills to make religious He makes religious; and had He willed it He would have made the Samaritans devout instead of indevout."

But the intrinsic cause of devotion on our part is meditation or contemplation. For, as we have said, devotion is a certain act of the will by which a man gives himself promptly to the Divine service. All acts of the will, however, proceed from consideration, since the will's object is good understood. Hence S. Augustine says: "The will starts from the understanding." Meditation must, then, be the cause of devotion inasmuch as it is from meditation that a man conceives the idea of giving himself up to God.

And two considerations lead a man to do this: one is the consideration of the Divine Goodness and of His benefits, whence the words of the Psalmist: *But for me it is good to cling close to my God, to put my hope in the Lord God.* And this consideration begets love, which is the proximate cause of devotion. And the second is man's consideration of his own defects which compel him to lean upon God, according to the words: *I have lifted up mine eyes to the mountains, from whence help shall come to me; my help is from the Lord Who made Heaven and earth.* This latter consideration excludes all presumption which, by making him lean upon himself, might prevent a man from submitting himself to God.

Some, however, argue that contemplation or meditation is not the cause of devotion, thus:

1. No cause hinders its own effect. But subtle intellectual meditations often hinder devotion.

But it is the consideration of those things which naturally tend to excite love of God which begets devotion; consideration of things which do not come under this head, but rather distract the mind from it, are a hindrance to devotion.

2. Again, if contemplation were the real cause of devotion, it should follow that the higher the matter of our contemplation the greater the devotion it begot. But the opposite is the case. For it frequently happens that greater devotion is aroused by the contemplation of the Passion of Christ and of the other mysteries of His Sacred Humanity than by meditation upon the Divine excellences.

It is true that things which concern the Godhead are of themselves more calculated to excite in us love, and consequently devotion, since God is to be loved above all things; yet it is due to the weakness of the human mind that just as it needs to be led by the hand to the knowledge of Divine things, so also must it be lead to Divine love by means of the things of sense already known to it; and the chief of these things is the Humanity of Christ, as is said in the *Preface* of the Mass: *So that knowing God visibly in the flesh, we may thereby be carried away to the love of things invisible.* Consequently the things that have to do with Christ's Humanity lead us, as it were, by the hand and are thus especially suited to stir up devotion in us; though, none the less, devotion is principally concerned with the Divinity.

3. Lastly, if contemplation were the real cause of devotion, it ought to follow that those who are the more fitted for contemplation are also the more fitted for devotion; whereas the contrary is the case, for greater devotion is often found among simple folk and in the female sex, where contemplation is wanting.

But knowledge, as indeed anything which renders a person great, occasions a man to trust in Himself, and hence he does not wholly give himself to God. It is for this reason that knowledge and suchlike things are sometimes a hindrance to a man's devotion, whereas among women and simple folk devotion abounds by the suppression of all elation. But if a man will only perfectly subject to God his knowledge and any other perfection he may have, then his devotion will increase.

*Cajetan:* Note these two intrinsic causes of devotion: one, namely, which arises from meditation upon God and His benefits, the other from meditation on our own defects. Under the first head I must consider God's goodness, mercy, and kindness towards mankind and towards myself; the benefits, for instance, of creation according to His own Likeness, of Redemption, of Baptism, of His inspirations, of His invitations—whether directly or through the medium of others; His patient waiting till I do penance; His Holy Eucharist; His preserving me from so many perils both of body and soul; His care of me by means of His Angels; and His other individual benefits. Under the second head come all my faults and the punishments due to me, whether in the past or now in the present; my proneness to sin; my misuse of my own powers by habituating my thoughts and desires—as well as the inclinations of my other various faculties—to evil; my sojourning in a region far away from His Friendship and from His Divine conversation; my perverted affections which make me think far more of temporal than of spiritual advantages or disadvantages; my utter lack of virtue; the wounds of my ignorance, of my malice, of my weakness, of my concupiscence; the shackles on my hands and feet, on my good works, that is; the shackles, too, on my affections, so that I dwell amidst darkness and rottenness and bitterness, and shrink not from it! My deafness, too, to the inner voice of my Shepherd; and, what is far worse, that I have chosen God for my enemy and my adversary as often as I have chosen mortal sin, and that I have thus offered Him the grievous insult of refusing to have Him for my God, and choosing instead my belly, or money, or false delights—and called them my God!

Meditations such as these should be in daily use among spiritual and religious people, and for their sake they should put aside the "much-speaking" of vocal prayer, however much it may appeal to them. And it is of such meditations that devotion and, by consequence, other virtues, are begotten. And they who do not give themselves to this form of prayer at least once in the day cannot be called religious men or women, nor even spiritual people. There can be no effect without a cause, no end without means to it, no gaining the harbour on the island save by a voyage in a ship; and so there can be no real religion without repeated acts regarding its causes, the means to it, and the vehicle that is to bring us thither (*on* 2. 2. 82. 3).

*Cajetan:* Just as he who removes an obstacle is the occasion of the resulting effect—a man, for instance, who pulls down a pillar is the occasion of the resulting fall of what it supported, and a man who removes a water-dam is the occasion of the consequent flood—so in the same way have women and simple folk a cause of devotion within themselves, for they have not that obstacle which consists in self-confidence. And because God bestows His grace on those who put no obstacle to it, the Church therefore calls the female sex "devout." Hence we are not to find fault with the learned for their knowledge, nor are we to praise women for womanly weakness; but that abuse of knowledge which consists in self-exaltation is blameworthy, just as the right use of women's weakness in not being uplifted is praiseworthy (*on* 2. 2. 82. 3).

IV

Is Joy an Effect of Devotion?

In the Church's *Collect* for the Thursday after the Fourth Sunday of Lent we say: *May holy devotion fill with joy those whom the fast they have undertaken chastises.*

Of itself indeed, and primarily, devotion brings about a spiritual joy of the mind; but as an accidental result it causes sorrow. For, as we have said above, devotion arises from two considerations. Primarily it arises from the consideration of the Divine Goodness, and from this thought there necessarily follows gladness, in accordance with the words: *I remembered God and was delighted.* Yet, as it were accidentally, this consideration begets a certain sadness in those who do not as yet fully enjoy God: *My soul hath thirsted after the strong living God*, and he immediately adds: *My tears have been my bread.*

Secondly, however, devotion arises from the consideration of our own defects, for we thus reflect upon that from which a man, by devout acts of the will, turns away, so as no longer to dwell in himself, but to subject himself to God.

And this consideration is the converse of the former: for of itself it tends to cause sadness since it makes us dwell upon our defects; accidentally, however, it causes joy, for it makes us think of the hope we have of God's assistance.

Hence joy of heart primarily and of itself follows from devotion; but secondarily and accidentally there results a sadness which is unto God.

Some, however, argue that joy is not an effect of devotion, thus:

1. Christ's Passion, as said before, is especially calculated to cause devotion. But from dwelling on it there follows a certain affliction of soul: *Remember my poverty ... the wormwood and the gall*—that is, the Sacred Passion; and then follows: *I will be mindful, and remember, and my soul shall languish within me.*

In meditation on the Passion of Christ there is food for sadness—viz., the thought of the sins of men, and to take these away Christ had need to suffer. But there is also food for joy—viz., the thought of God's merciful kindness towards us in providing us such a deliverance.

2. Again, devotion principally consists in the interior sacrifice of the heart: *A sacrifice to God is an afflicted spirit*; consequently affliction, rather than pleasure or joy, is the outcome of devotion.

But the soul which is on the one hand saddened because of its shortcomings in this present life, is on the other hand delighted at the thought of the goodness of God and of the hope of Divine assistance.

3. Lastly, S. Gregory of Nyssa says: "Just as laughter proceeds from joy, so are sorrow and groaning signs of sadness." But out of devotion some burst into tears.

Yet tears spring not from sadness alone, but also from a certain tenderness of feeling: and especially is this the case when we reflect on something that, while pleasant, has in it a certain admixture of sadness; thus men are wont to weep from loving affection when they recover their children or others dear to them whom they had thought lost. And it is in this sense that tears spring from devotion.

*Cajetan:* Notice the proof here afforded that those are not devout persons who are habitually sad and gloomy, and who cannot mingle with others without getting into difficulties or dissolving into tears. For devout folk are cheerful, and are full of joy in their souls; and this not solely by reason of the principal cause, as is stated in the text, but also by reason of a secondary cause—the thought, namely, of their own failings. For the sadness of devout folk is *according to God*, and joy accompanies it; whence S. Augustine's remark: "Let a man grieve, but let him rejoice at his grief." Therefore it is that we read of the Saints that they were joyful and bright; and rightly so, for they had begun upon earth their "heavenly conversation" (*on* 2. 2. 82. 4).

*S. Augustine:* For Thee do I yearn, Justice and Innocence, Beautiful and Fair in Thy beauteous light that satisfies and yet never sates! For with Thee is repose exceedingly and life without disquiet! He that enters into Thee enters into the joy of his Lord; he shall know no fear, and in the Best shall be best. But I have deserted Thee and have wandered away, O Lord, my God! Too far have I wandered from Thee, the Steadfast One, in my youth, and I have become to myself a very land of want! (*Confessions*, II. x.).

QUESTION LXXXIII

OF PRAYER

I

Is Prayer an Act of the Appetitive Powers?

S. Isidore says: "To pray is the same thing as to speak." Speaking, however, belongs to the intellect. Hence prayer is not an act of the appetitive, but of the intellectual faculties.

According to Cassiodorus, on those words of the Psalmist: *Hear my prayer, O Lord, and my supplication, give ear to my tears*, prayer means "the lips' reasoning." Now there is this difference between the speculative and the practical reason, that the speculative reason merely apprehends things, while the practical reason not only apprehends things, but actually causes them. But one thing is the cause of another in two ways: in one way, perfectly—namely, as inducing a necessity—as happens when the effect comes entirely under the power of a cause; in another way, imperfectly—namely, by merely disposing to it—as happens when an effect is not entirely under the power of a cause.

And so, too, reason is in two ways the cause of certain things: in one way as imposing a necessity; and in this way it belongs to the reason to command not merely the lower faculties and the bodily members, but even men who are subject to us, and this is done by giving commands. In another way as inducing, and in some sort disposing to, an effect; and in this way the reason asks for something to be done by those who are subject to it, whether they be equals or superiors.

But both of these—namely, to command something, or to ask or beg for something to be done—imply a certain arrangement—as when a man arranges for something to be done by somebody else. And in this respect both of these acts come under the reason whose office it is to arrange. Hence the Philosopher says: "Reason asks for the best things."

Here, then, we speak of prayer as implying a certain asking or petition, for, as S. Augustine says: "Prayer is a certain kind of petition"; so, too, S. John Damascene says: "Prayer is the asking of fitting things from God."

Hence it is clear that the prayer of which we are here speaking is an act of the reason.

Some, however, think that prayer is an act of the appetitive powers, thus:

I. The whole object of prayer is to be heard, and the Psalmist says that it is our desires which are heard: *The Lord hath heard the desire of the poor.* Prayer, then, is desire; but desire is an act of the appetitive powers.

But the Lord is said to hear the desires of the poor either because their desire is the reason why they ask—since our petitions are in a certain sense the outward expression of our desires;

or this may be said in order to show the swiftness with which He hears them—even while things are only existing in the poor man's desire; God hears them even before they are expressed in prayer. And this accords with the words of Isaias: *And it shall come to pass that before they shall call I will hear, as they are yet speaking I will hear.*

2. Again, Denis the Areopagite says: "But before all things it is good to begin with prayer, as thereby giving ourselves up to and uniting ourselves with God." But union with God comes through love, and love belongs to the appetitive powers; therefore prayer, too, would seem to belong to the appetitive powers.

But the will moves the reason to its end or object. Hence there is nothing to prevent the reason, under the direction of the will, from tending to the goal of charity, which is union with God. Prayer, however, tends towards God—moved, that is, by the will, which itself is motived by charity—in two ways: in one way by reason of that which is asked for, since in prayer we have particularly to ask that we may be united with God, according to those words: *One thing I have asked of the Lord, this will I seek after, that I may dwell in the house of the Lord all the days of my life.* And in another way prayer tends towards God—by reason, namely, of the petitioner himself; for such a one must approach him from whom he asks something, and this either bodily, as when he draws nigh to a man, or mentally, as when he draws nigh to God.

Hence the same Denis says: "When we invoke God in prayer we are before Him with our minds laid bare." In the same sense S. John Damascene says: "Prayer is the ascent of the mind towards God." *Cajetan:* Prayer demands of the petitioner a twofold union with God: the one is general—the union, that is, of friendship—and is produced by charity, so that further on we shall find the friendship arising from charity enumerated among the conditions for infallibly efficacious prayer. The second kind of union may be termed substantial union; it is the effect of prayer itself. It is that union of application by which the mind offers itself and all it has to God in service—viz., by devout affections, by meditations, and by external acts. By such union as this a man who prays is inseparable from God in his worship and service, just as when one man serves another he is inseparable from him in his service (*on* 2. 2. 83. 1).

"And now, O Lord, Thou art our Father, and we are clay: and Thou art our Maker, and we are all the works of Thy hands. Be not very angry, O Lord, and remember no longer our iniquity: behold, see we are all Thy people."

II

Is It Fitting To Pray?

In S. Luke's Gospel we read: *We ought always to pray and not to faint.*

A threefold error regarding prayer existed amongst the ancients; for some maintained that human affairs were not directed by Divine Providence; whence it followed that it was altogether vain to pray or to worship God; of such we read: *You have said, he laboureth in vain that serveth God.* A second opinion was that all things, even human affairs, happened of necessity—whether from the immutability of Divine Providence, or from a necessity imposed by the stars, or from the connection of causes; and this opinion, of course, excluded all utility from prayer. A third opinion was that human affairs were indeed directed by Divine Providence, and that human affairs did not happen of necessity, but that Divine Providence was changeable, and that consequently its dispositions were changed by our prayers and by other acts of religious worship. These views, however, have elsewhere been shown to be wrong.

Consequently we have so to set forth the utility of prayer as neither to make things happen of necessity because subject to Divine Providence, nor to suggest that the arrangements of Divine Providence are subject to change.

To bring this out clearly we must consider that Divine Providence not merely arranges what effects shall take place, but also from what causes they shall proceed, and in what order.

But amongst other causes human acts are causes of certain effects. Hence men must do certain things, not so that their acts may change the Divine arrangement, but that by their acts they may bring about certain effects according to the order arranged by God; and it is the same with natural causes. It is the same, too, in the case of prayer. For we do not pray in order to change the Divine arrangements, but in order to win that which God arranged should be fulfilled by means of prayers; or, in S. Gregory's words: "Men by petitioning may merit to receive what Almighty God arranged before the ages to give them."

Some, however, maintain that prayer is futile, thus:

1. Prayer seems to be necessary in order that we may bring our wants to the notice of Him to Whom we make the petition. But our Lord says: *Your Father knoweth that ye have need of all these things.*

But it is not necessary for us to set forth our petitions before God in order to make known to Him our needs or desires, but rather that we ourselves may realize that in these things it is needful to have recourse to the Divine assistance.

2. Again, by prayer the mind of him to whom it is made is prevailed upon to grant what is asked of him; but the mind of God is unchangeable and inflexible: *The Triumpher in Israel will not spare, and will not be moved to repentance; for He is not a man that He should repent.* Consequently it is unavailing to pray to God.

But our prayers do not aim at changing the Divine arrangements, but at obtaining by our prayers what God has arranged to give us.

3. Lastly, it is more generous to give to one who does not ask than to one who asks, for, as Seneca remarks: "Nothing is bought at a dearer price than what is bought with prayers." Whereas God is most generous.

God, indeed, bestows on us many things out of His generosity, even things for which we do not ask; but He wishes to grant us some things on the supposition that we ask for them. And this is for our advantage, for it is intended to beget in us a certain confidence in having recourse to God, as well as to make us recognize that He is the Author of all good to us. Hence S. Chrysostom says: "Reflect what great happiness is bestowed upon you, what glory is given you, namely, to converse in your prayers with God, to join in colloquy with Christ, and to beg for what you wish or desire."

*Cajetan:* Notice how foolish are some Christians who, when desirous of reaching certain ends attainable by nature or art, are most careful to apply such means, and would rightly regard their hopes as vain unless they applied them; and yet at the same time they have quite false notions of the fruits to be derived from prayer: as though prayer were no cause at all, or at least but a remote one! Whence it comes to pass that, having false ideas about the causes, they fail to reap any fruit (*on* 2. 2. 83. 2).

*S. Augustine:* But some may say: It is not so much a question whether we are to pray by words or deeds as whether we are to pray at all if God already knows what is needful for us. Yet the very giving ourselves to prayer has the effect of soothing our minds and purifying them; it makes us more fit to receive the Divine gifts which are spiritually poured out upon us. For God does not hear us because of a display of prayer on our part; He is always ready, indeed, to give us His light, not, indeed, His visible light, but the light of the intellect and the spirit. It is we who are not always prepared to receive it, and this because we are preoccupied with other things and swallowed up in the darkness resulting from desire of the things of earth. When we pray, then, our hearts must turn to God, Who is ever ready to give if only we will take what He gives. And in so turning to Him we must purify the eye of our mind by shutting out all thought for the things of time, that so—with single-minded gaze—we may be able to bear that simple light that shines divinely, and neither sets nor changes. And not merely to bear it, but even to abide in it; and this not simply without strain, but with a certain unspeakable joy. In this joy the life of the Blessed is truly and really perfected (*On the Sermon on the Mount*, II. iii. 14).

*S. Augustine:* He could have bestowed these things on us even without our prayers; but He wished that by our prayers we should be taught from Whom these benefits come. For from whom do we receive them if not from Him from Whom we are bidden to ask them? Assuredly in this matter the Church does not demand laborious disputations; but note Her daily prayers: She prays that unbelievers may believe: God then brings them to the Faith. She prays that the faithful may persevere: God gives them perseverance to the end. And God foreknew that He would do these things. For this is the predestination of the Saints whom *He chose in Christ before the foundation of the world* (*Of the Gift of Perseverance*, vii. 15).

"Thou hast taught me, O God, from my youth; and till now I will declare Thy wonderful works. And unto old age and grey hairs, O God, forsake me not, until I shew forth Thy arm to all the generation that is to come."

III

Is Prayer an Act of the Virtue of Religion?

In Ps. cxl. 2 we read: *Let my prayer be directed as incense in Thy sight*, and on these words the Gloss remarks: "According to this figure, in the Old Law incense was said to be offered as an odour of sweetness to the Lord." And this comes under the virtue of religion. Therefore prayer is an act of religion.

It properly belongs to the virtue of religion to give due reverence and honour to God, and hence all those things by which such reverence is shown to God come under religion. By prayer, however, a man shows reverence to God inasmuch as he submits himself to Him and, by praying, acknowledges that he needs God as the Author of all his good. Whence it is clear that prayer is properly an act of religion.

Some, however, maintain that prayer is not an act of the virtue of religion, thus:

1. Prayer is rather the exercise of the Gift of Understanding than of the virtue of religion. For the virtue of religion comes under Justice; it is therefore resident in the will. But prayer belongs to the intellectual faculties, as we have shown above.

But we must remember that the will moves the other faculties of the soul to their objects or ends, and that consequently the virtue of religion, which is in the will, directs the acts of the other faculties in the reverence they show towards God. Now amongst these other faculties of the soul the intellect is the noblest and the most nigh to the will; consequently, next to devotion, which belongs to the will itself, prayer, which belongs to the intellective part, is the chief act of religion, for by it religion moves a man's understanding towards God.

2. Again, acts of worship fall under precept, whereas prayer seems to fall under no precept, but to proceed simply from the mere wish to pray; for prayer is merely asking for what we want; consequently prayer is not an act of the virtue of religion.

Yet not only to ask for what we desire, but to desire rightly, falls under precept; to desire, indeed, falls under the precept of charity, but to ask falls under the precept of religion—the precept which is laid down in the words: *Ask and ye shall receive*.

3. Lastly, the virtue of religion embraces due worship and ceremonial offered to the Divinity; prayer, however, offers God nothing, but only seeks to obtain things from Him.

In prayer a man offers to God his mind, which he subjects to Him in reverence, and which he, in some sort, lays bare before Him—as we have just seen in S. Denis's words. Hence, since the human mind is superior to all the other exterior or bodily members, and also to all exterior things which have place in the Divine worship, it follows that prayer, too, is pre-eminent among the acts of the virtue of religion.

*Cajetan:* In prayer or petition there are three things to be considered: the thing petitioned for, the actual petition, and the petitioner. As far, then, as the thing petitioned for is concerned, we give nothing to God when we pray; rather we ask Him to give us something. But if we consider the actual petition, then we do offer something to God when we pray. For the very act of petitioning is an act of subjection; it is an acknowledgment of God's power. And the proof of this is that proud men would prefer to submit to want rather than humble themselves by asking anything of others. Further, the petitioner, by the very fact that he petitions, acknowledges that he whom he petitions has the power to assist him, and is merciful, or just, or provident; it is for this reason that he hopes to be heard. Hence petition or prayer is regarded as an act of the virtue of religion, the object of which is to give honour to God. For we honour God by asking things of Him, and this by so much the more as—whether from our manner of asking or from the nature of what we ask for—we acknowledge Him to be above all things, to be our Creator, our Provider, our Redeemer, etc. And this is what S. Thomas points out in the body of the Article. But if we consider the petitioner: then, since man petitions with his mind—for petition is an act of the mind—and since the mind is the noblest thing in man, it follows that by petitioning we submit to God that which is noblest in us, since we use it to ask things of Him, and thereby do Him honour. Thus by prayer we offer our minds in sacrifice to God; so, too, by bending the knee to Him we offer to Him and sacrifice to Him our knees, by using them to His honour (*on* 2. 2. 83. 3).

*S. Augustine:* I stand as a beggar at the gate, He sleepeth not on Whom I call! Oh, may He give me those three loaves! For you remember the Gospel? Ah! see how good a thing it is to know God's word; those of you who have read it are stirred within yourselves! For you remember how a needy man came to his friend's house and asked for three loaves. And He says that he sleepily replied to him: "I am resting, and my children are with me asleep." But he persevered in his request, and wrung from him by his importunity what his deserts could not get. But God wishes to give; yet only to those who ask—lest He should give to those who understand not. He does not wish to be stirred up by your weariness! For when you pray you are not being troublesome to one who sleeps; *He slumbereth not nor sleeps that keepeth Israel.* ... He, then, sleeps not; see you that your faith sleeps not! (*Enarr. in Ps.* cii. 10).

*S. Augustine:* Some there are who either do not pray at all, or pray but tepidly; and this because, forsooth, they have learnt from the Lord Himself that God knows, even before we ask Him, what is necessary for us. But because of such folk are we to say that these words are not true and therefore to be blotted out of the Gospel? Nay, rather, since it is clear that God gives some things even to those who do not ask—as, for instance, the beginnings of faith—and has prepared other things for those only who pray for them—as, for instance, final perseverance—it is evident that he who fancies he has this latter of himself does not pray to have it (*Of the Gift of Perseverance*, xvi. 39).

"I will sing to the Lord as long as I live; I will sing praise to my God while I have my being. Let my speech be acceptable to Him; but I will take delight in the Lord."

IV

Ought We To Pray To God Alone?

In Job v. 1 we read: *Call, now, if there be any that will answer thee, and turn to some of the Saints.*

Prayer is addressed to a person in two ways: in one way as a petition to be granted by him; in another way as a petition to be forwarded by him. In the former way we only pray to God, for all our prayers ought to be directed to the attaining of grace and glory, and these God alone gives: *The Lord will give grace and glory.* But in the latter way we set forth our prayers both to the holy Angels and to men; and this, not that through their intervention God may know our petitions, but rather that by their prayers and merits our petitions may gain their end. Hence it is said in the Apocalypse: *And the smoke of the incense of the prayers of the Saints ascended up before God from the hand of the Angel.* And this is clearly shown, too, from the style adopted by the Church in her prayers: for of the Holy Trinity we pray that mercy may be shown us; but of all the Saints, whomsoever they may be, we pray that they may intercede for us.

Some, however, maintain that we ought to pray to God alone, thus:

1. Prayer is an act of the virtue of religion. But only God is to be worshipped by the virtue of religion. Consequently it is to Him alone that we should pray.

But in our prayers we only show religious worship to Him from Whom we hope to obtain what we ask, for by so doing we confess Him to be the Author of all our goods; but we do not show religious worship to those whom we seek to have as intercessors with us before God.

2. Again, prayer to those who cannot know what we pray for is idle. But God alone can know our prayers, and this because prayer is frequently a purely interior act of which God alone is cognizant, as the Apostle says: *I will pray with the spirit, I will pray also with the understanding;* and also because, as S. Augustine says: The dead know not, not even the Saints, what the living—not even excepting their own children—are doing.

It is true that the dead, if we consider only their natural condition, do not know what is done on earth, and especially do they not know the interior movements of the heart. But to the Blessed, as S. Gregory says, manifestation is made in the Divine Word of those things which it is fitting that they should know as taking place in our regard, even the interior movements of the heart. And, indeed, it is most befitting their state of excellence that they should be cognizant of petitions addressed to them, whether vocally or mentally. Hence through God's revelation they are cognizant of the petitions which we address them.

3. Lastly, some say: if we do address prayers to any of the Saints, the sole reason for doing so lies in the fact that they are closely united to God. But we do not address prayers to people who, while still living in this world, are closely knit to God, nor to those who are in Purgatory and are united to Him. There seems, then, to be no reason why we should address prayers to the Saints in Paradise. But they who are still in the world or in Purgatory do not as yet enjoy the vision of the Divine Word so as to be able to know what we think or say, hence we do not implore their help when we pray; though when talking with living people we do ask them to help us.

*S. Augustine:* It is no great thing to live long, nor even to live for ever; but it is indeed a great thing to live well. Oh, let us love eternal life! And we realize how earnestly we ought to strive for that eternal life when we note how men who love this present temporal life so work for it—though it is to pass away—that, when the fear of death comes, they strive all they can, not, indeed, to do away with death, but to put death off! How men labour when death approaches! They flee from it; they hide from it; they give all they have; they try to buy themselves off; they work and strive; they put up with tortures and inconveniences; they call in physicians; they do everything that lies within their power! Yet even if they spend all their toil and their substance, they can only secure that they may live a little longer, not that they may live for ever! If, then, men spend such toil, such endeavour, so much money, so much anxiety, watchfulness, and care, in order to live only a little longer, what ought we not to do that we may live for ever? And if we call them prudent who take every possible precaution to stave off death, to live but a few days more, to save just a few days, then how foolish are they who so pass their days as to lose the Day of Eternity! (*Sermon*, cxxvii. 2).

"May God have mercy on us, and bless us: may He cause the light of His countenance to shine upon us, and may He have mercy on us. That we may know Thy way upon earth: Thy salvation in all nations. Let people confess to Thee, O God: let all people give praise to Thee. Let the nations be glad and rejoice: for Thou judgest the people with justice, and directest the nations upon earth. Let the people, O God, confess to Thee: let all the people give praise to Thee: the earth hath yielded her fruit. May God, our God bless us, may God bless us: and all the ends of the earth fear Him."

V

Should We in our Prayers ask for Anything Definite from God?

Our Lord taught the disciples to ask definitely for the things which are contained in the petitions of the Lord's Prayer: *Thus shalt thou pray.*

Maximus Valerius tells of Socrates that he "maintained that nothing further should be asked of the immortal gods save that they should give us good things; and this on the ground that they knew well what was best for each individual, whereas we often ask in our prayers for things which it would be better not to have asked for." And this opinion has some truth in it as regards those things which can turn out ill, or which a man can use well or ill, as, for example, riches which, as the same Socrates says, "have been to the destruction of many; or honours which have ruined many; or the possession of kingdoms, the issues of which are so often ill-fated; or splendid matrimonial alliances, which have sometimes proved the ruin of families." But there are certain good things of which a man cannot make a bad use—those, namely, which cannot have a bad issue. And these are the things by which we are rendered blessed and by which we merit beatitude; these are the things for which the Saints pray unconditionally: *Show us Thy Face and we shall be saved*; and again: *Lead me along the path of Thy commandments.*

Some, however, say that we ought not in our prayers to ask for definite things from God, thus:

1. S. John Damascene defines prayer as "asking from God things that are fitting"; consequently prayer for things which are not expedient is of no efficacy, as S. James says: *You ask and receive not, because you ask amiss.* Moreover, S. Paul says: *We know not what we should pray for as we ought.*

But it is also true that though a man cannot of himself know what he ought to pray for, yet, as the Apostle says in the same place: *In this the Spirit helpeth our infirmity*—namely, in that, by inspiring us with holy desires, He makes us ask aright. Hence Our Lord says that the true adorers *must adore in spirit and in truth.*

2. Further, he who asks from another some definite thing strives to bend that other's will to do what the petitioner wants. But we ought not to direct our prayers towards making God will what we will, but rather we should will what He wills—as the Gloss says on the words of Ps. xxxii. 1: *Rejoice in the Lord, O ye just!* It would seem, therefore, that we ought not to ask for definite things from God when we pray.

Yet when in our prayers we ask for things which appertain to our salvation, we are conforming our will to the will of God, for of His will it is said: *He will have all men to be saved.*

3. Lastly, evil things cannot be asked from God; and He Himself invites us to receive good things. But it is idle for a person to ask for what he is invited to receive.

God, it is true, invites us to receive good things; but He wishes us to come to them—not, indeed, by the footsteps of the body—but by pious desires and devout prayers.

*S. Augustine:* Fly, then, by unwavering faith and holy habits, fly, brethren, from those torments where the torturers never desist, and where the tortured never die; whose death is unending, and where in their anguish they cannot die. But burn with love for and desire of the eternal life of the Saints where there is no longer the life of toil nor yet wearisome repose. For the praises of God will beget no disgust, neither will they ever cease. There will there be no weariness of the soul, no bodily fatigue; there will there be no wants: neither wants of your own which will call for succour, nor wants of your neighbour demanding your speedy help. God will be all your delight; there will ye find the abundance of that Holy City that from Him draws life and happily and wisely lives in Him. For there, according to that promise of His for which we hope and wait, we shall be made equal to the Angels of God; and equally with them shall we then enjoy that vision of the Holy Trinity in which we now but walk by faith. For we now believe what we do not see, that so by the merits of that same faith we then may merit to see what we believe, and may so hold fast to it that the Equality of Father, Son, and Holy Ghost, and the Unity of the Trinity, may no longer come to us under the garb of faith, nor be the subject of contentious talk, but may rather be what we may drink in in purest and deepest contemplation amid the silence of Eternity (*De Catechizandis Rudibus*, xxv. 47).

*S. Augustine:* O Lord, my God, give me what Thou biddest and then bid what Thou wilt! Thou biddest us be continent. *And I knew*, as a certain one says, *that I could not otherwise be continent save God gave it, and this also was a point of wisdom to know Whose gift it was.* Now by continence we are knit together and brought back into union with that One from Whom we have wandered away after many things. For he loves Thee but little who loves other things with Thee, and loves them not for Thee! O Love that ever burnest and wilt never be extinguished! O Charity! O Lord, my God, set me on fire! Thou dost bid continence? Then give me what Thou biddest and bid what Thou wilt! (*Confessions*, X. xxix.).

*S. Augustine:* O Lord, my God, listen to my prayer and mercifully hear my desire! For my desire burns not for myself alone, but fraternal charity bids it be of use. And Thou seest in my heart that it is so; for I would offer to Thee in sacrifice the service of my thoughts and of my tongue. Grant me then what I may offer to Thee. For I am needy and poor, and Thou art rich towards all that call upon Thee; for in peace and tranquillity hast Thou care for us. Circumcise, then, my lips, within and without, from all rashness and all untruthfulness. May Thy Scriptures be my chaste delight; may I never be deceived in them nor deceive others out of them. Attend, O Lord, and have mercy upon me, O Lord, my God. Thou art the Light of the blind, the Strength of the weak, and so, too, art Thou the Light of them that see and the Strength of them that are strong. Look, then, on my soul, and hear me when I cry from out the depths! (*Confessions*, XI. ii. 2).

"Look down from Heaven, and behold from Thy holy habitation and the place of Thy glory: where is Thy zeal, and Thy strength, the multitude of Thy bowels, and of Thy mercies? they have held back themselves from me. For Thou art our Father, and Abraham hath not known us, and Israel hath been ignorant of us: Thou, O Lord, art our Father, our Redeemer, from everlasting is Thy Name."

VI

Ought We in our Prayers to ask for Temporal Things from God?

We have the authority of the Book of Proverbs for answering in the affirmative, for there we read: *Give me only the necessaries of life*.

S. Augustine says to Proba: "It is lawful to pray for what it is lawful to desire." But it is lawful to desire temporal things, not indeed as our principal aim or as something which we make our end, but rather as props and stays which may be of assistance to us in our striving for the possession of God; for by such things our bodily life is sustained, and such things, as the Philosopher says, co-operate organically to the production of virtuous acts. Consequently it is lawful to pray for temporal things. And this is what S. Augustine means when he says to Proba: "Not unfittingly does a person desire sufficiency for this life when he desires it and nothing more; for such sufficiency is not sought for its own sake but for the body's health, and for a mode of life suitable to a man's position so that he may not be a source of inconvenience to those with whom he lives. When, then, we have these things we must pray that we may retain them, and when we have not got them we must pray that we may have them."

Some, however, argue that we ought not to pray for temporal things, thus:

1. What we pray for we seek. But we are forbidden to seek for temporal things, for it is said: *Seek ye therefore first the kingdom of God, and His justice, and all these things shall be added unto you*, those temporal things, namely, which He says are not to be sought but which are to be added to the things which we seek.

But temporal things are to be sought secondarily not primarily. Hence S. Augustine: "When He says the former is *to be sought first* (namely the kingdom of God), He means that the latter (namely temporal good things) are to be sought afterwards; not *afterwards* in point of time, but *afterwards* in point of importance; the former as our good, the latter as our need."

2. Again, we only ask for things about which we are solicitous. But we are not allowed to be solicitous about temporal concerns: *Be not solicitous for your life, what ye shall eat....*

But not all solicitude about temporal affairs is forbidden, only such as is superfluous and out of due order.

3. Further, we ought in prayer to uplift our minds to God. But by asking for temporal things in prayer our mind descends to things beneath it, and this is contrary to the teaching of the Apostle: *While we look not at the things which are seen, but at the things which are not seen. For the things which are seen are temporal: but the things which are not seen are eternal*.

When our mind is occupied with temporal affairs so as to set up its rest in them then it remains in them, and is depressed by them; but when the mind turns to them as a means of attaining to eternal life it is not depressed by them, but rather uplifted by them.

4. Lastly, men ought not to pray except for things useful and good. But temporal possessions are at times hurtful, and this not merely spiritually but even temporally; hence a man ought not to ask them of God.

But it is clear that since we do not seek temporal things primarily or for their own sake, but with reference to something else, we consequently only ask them of God according as they may be expedient for our salvation.

*S. Augustine: Lord, all my desire is before Thee, and my groaning is not hid from Thee!* It is not before men who cannot see the heart, but *before Thee is all my desire!* And let your desires, too, be before Him, and your Father Who seeth in secret will repay thee. For your very desire is a prayer, and if your desire is continual your prayer, too, is continual. Not without reason did the Apostle say: *Pray without ceasing.* Yet can we genuflect without ceasing? Can we prostrate without ceasing? Can we lift up our hands without ceasing? How, then, does he say: *Pray without ceasing?* If by *prayer* he meant such things as these then I think we could not pray without ceasing. But there is another prayer, an interior prayer, which is without ceasing—*desire.* Whatever else you do, if only you desire that *rest* you cease not to pray. If you wish to pray without ceasing then desire without ceasing. Your continual desire is your continual voice; but you will be silent if you cease to love (*Enarr. in Ps.* xxxvii. 10).

*S. Augustine:* But all these things are the gifts of my God; I did not give them to myself; they are good, and all these things am I. He then is good Who made me; nay, He Himself is my Good, and in Him do I rejoice for all the good things which I had even as a boy! But in this did I sin that, not in Him but in His creatures did I seek myself and other pleasures, high thoughts and truths. Thus it was that I fell into sorrow, confusion, and error. Thanks be to Thee, my Sweetness, my Honour and my Trust, O my God! Thanks be to Thee for Thy gifts! But do Thou keep them for me! For so doing Thou wilt be keeping me, and those things which Thou hast given me will be increased and perfected, and I myself shall be with Thee, for even that I should be at all is Thy gift to me! (*Confessions*, I. xx. 2).

*S. Augustine:* But I forget not, neither will I keep silence regarding the severity of Thy scourge and the wondrous swiftness of Thy mercy. Thou didst torture me with toothache; and when the pain had become so great that I could not even speak, it came into my mind to tell all my friends who were there to pray to Thee for me, to Thee the God of all manner of succour. And I wrote my request on a wax tablet and I gave it them to read. And hardly had we bent the knee in humble prayer than the pain fled! But what a pain it was! And how did it disappear? I was terrified, I confess it, O Lord my God! Never in all my life had I felt anything like it! (*Confessions*, IX. iv. 12).

It is narrated of S. Thomas that when at Paris it happened that having to lecture at the University on a subject which he had commenced the day before, he rose at night to pray as was his wont, but discovered that a tooth had suddenly pushed its way through his gums in such a way that he could not speak. His companion suggested that since it was an inopportune time for procuring assistance a message should be sent to the University stating what had happened and pointing out that the lecture could not be given till the tooth had been removed by a surgeon. But S. Thomas, reflecting upon the difficulty in which the University would be placed, considering also the danger which might arise from the removal of the tooth in the way suggested, said to his companion: I see no remedy save to trust to God's Providence. He then betook himself to his accustomed place of prayer, and for a long space besought God with tears to grant him this favour, leaving himself entirely in His hands. And when he had thus prayed he took the tooth between his fingers, and it came out at once without the slightest pain or wrench, and he found himself freed from the impediment to his speech which it had caused. This tooth he carried about with him for a long time as a reminder of an act of Divine loving-kindness such as he was anxious not to forget, for forgetfulness is the mother of ingratitude; he wished it, too, to move him to still greater confidence in the power of prayer which had on that occasion been so quickly heard (see *Vita S. Thomæ*, Bollandists, March 7, vol. i., 1865, pp. 673, 704, 712).

*S. Augustine:* But temporal things are sometimes for our profit, sometimes for our hurt. For many poverty was good, wealth did them harm. For many a hidden life was best, high station did them harm. And on the other hand money was good for some, and dignities, too, were good for them—good, that is, for those who used them well; but such things did harm when not taken away from those who used them ill. Consequently, brethren, let us ask for these temporal things with moderation, being sure that if we do receive them, He gives them Who knoweth what is best suited to us. You have asked for something, then, and what you asked for has not been given you? Believe in your Father Who would give it you if it were expedient for you (*Sermon*, lxxx. 7).

*S. Augustine:* Sometimes God in His wrath grants what you ask; at other times in His mercy He refuses what you ask. When, then, you ask of Him things which He praises, which He commands, things which He has promised us in the next world, then ask in confidence and be instant in prayer as far as in you lies, that so you may receive what you ask. For such things as these are granted by the God of mercy; they flow not from His wrath but from His compassion. But when you ask for temporal things, then ask with moderation, ask with fear; leave all to Him so that if they be for your profit He may give them you, if they be to your hurt He may refuse them. For what is for our good and what is to our hurt the Physician knoweth, not the patient (*Sermon*, cccliv. 8).

"Cast thy care upon the Lord, and He shall sustain thee; He shall not suffer the just to waver for ever."

VII

Ought We To Pray for Others?

S. James, in his Epistle, says: *Pray for one another that ye may be saved*.

As we said above, we ought in prayer to ask for those things which we ought to desire. But we ought to desire good things not for ourselves only but also for others, for this belongs to that charity which we ought to exercise towards our neighbour. Hence charity demands that we pray for others. In accordance with this S. Chrysostom says: "Necessity compels us to pray for ourselves, fraternal charity urges us to pray for others. But that prayer is more pleasing before God which arises not so much from our needs as from the demands of fraternal charity."

Some, however, urge that we ought not to pray for others, thus:

1. We are bound in our prayer to follow the norm which our Lord delivered to us; but in the *Lord's Prayer* we pray for ourselves and not for others, for we say: *Give us this day our daily bread*, etc.

But S. Cyprian says: "We do not say *my* Father, but *our* Father, neither do we say Give *me*, but give *us*; and this because the Teacher of Unity did not wish prayer to be made privately, viz., that each should pray for himself alone; for He wished one to pray for all since He in His single Person had borne all."

2. Again, we pray in order to be heard; but one of the conditions for our prayer to be heard is that a man should pray for himself. Thus on the words: *If ye ask the Father anything in My Name He will give it you*, S. Augustine says: "All are heard for themselves, but not for all in general, hence He does not say simply: *He will give it*, but *He will give it you*."

But to pray for oneself is a condition attaching to prayer; not indeed a condition affecting its merit, but a condition which is necessary if we would ensure the attainment of what we ask. For it sometimes happens that prayer made for another does not avail even though it be devout and persevering and for things pertaining to a man's salvation; and this is because of the existence of some hindrance on the part of him for whom we pray, as we read in Jeremias: *If Moses and Samuel shall stand before Me, My soul is not towards this people*. None the less, such prayer will be meritorious on the part of him who prays, for he prays out of charity; thus on the words, *And my prayer shall be turned into my bosom*, the Interlinear Gloss has: "That is, and even though it avail not for them, yet shall I not be without my reward."

3. Lastly, we are forbidden to pray for others if they are wicked, according to the words: *Do not thou pray for this people ... and do not withstand Me, for I will not hear thee*. And, on the other hand, we ought not to pray for them if they are good, for in that case they will be heard when they pray for themselves.

But we have to pray even for sinners, that they may be converted, and for the good, that they may persevere and make progress. Our prayers for sinners, however, are not heard for all, but for some. For they are heard for those who are predestined, not for those who are foreknown as reprobate; just in the same way as when we correct our brethren, such corrections avail among the predestinate but not among the reprobate, according to the words: *No man can correct whom He hath despised.* Wherefore also it is said: *He that knoweth his brother to sin a sin that is not unto death, let him ask, and life shall be given to him who sinneth not to death.* But just as we can refuse to no one, as long as he liveth on this earth, the benefit of correction—for we cannot distinguish between the predestinate and the reprobate, as S. Augustine says—so neither can we refuse to anyone the suffrage of our prayers.

And for good men we have to pray, and this for a threefold reason: firstly, because the prayers of many are more easily heard; thus on the words: *I beseech ye therefore, help me in your prayers for me*, the Ordinary Gloss of S. Ambrose says: "Well does the Apostle ask his inferiors to pray for him; for even the very least become great when many in number, and when gathered together with one mind; and it is impossible that the prayers of many should not avail" to obtain, that is, what is obtainable. And secondly, that thanks may be returned by many for the benefits conferred by God upon the just, for these same benefits tend to the profit of many—as is evident from the Apostle's words to the Corinthians. And thirdly, that those who are greater may not therefore be proud, but may realize that they need the suffrages of their inferiors. "Father, I will that where I am they also whom Thou hast given Me may be with Me; that they may see My glory, which Thou hast given Me: because Thou hast loved Me before the foundation of the world."

VIII

Ought We To Pray for Our Enemies?

*But I say to you ... pray for them that persecute and calumniate you.*

To pray for others is a work of charity, as we have said above. Hence we are bound to pray for our enemies in the same way as we are bound to love them. We have already explained, in the *Treatise on Charity*, in what sense we are bound to love our enemies; namely, that we are bound to love their nature, not their fault; and that to love our enemies in general is of precept; to love them, however, individually, is not of precept save in the sense of being prepared to do so; a man, for instance, is bound to be ready to love an individual enemy and to help him in case of necessity, or if he comes to seek his pardon. But absolutely to love our individual enemies, and to assist them, belongs to perfection.

In the same way, then, it is necessary that in our general prayers for others we should not exclude our enemies. But to make special prayer for them belongs to perfection and is not necessary, save in some particular cases. Some, however, argue that we ought not to pray for our enemies, thus:

1. It is said in the Epistle to the Romans: *What things soever were written were written for our learning*. But in Holy Scripture we find many imprecations against enemies; thus, for instance: *Let all my enemies be ashamed, let them be turned back and be ashamed very speedily*. From which it would rather seem that we ought to pray against our enemies than for them.

But the imprecations which find place in Holy Scripture can be understood in four different ways: first of all according as the Prophets are wont "to predict the future under the figure of imprecations," as S. Augustine says; secondly, in that certain temporal evils are sometimes sent by God upon sinners for their amendment; thirdly, these denunciations may be understood, not as demanding the punishment of men themselves, but as directed against the kingdom of sin, in the sense that by men being corrected sin may be destroyed; fourthly, in that the Prophets conform their wills to the Divine Justice with regard to the damnation of sinners who persevere in their sin.

2. Further, to be revenged upon our enemies means evil for our enemies. But the Saints seek to be avenged upon their enemies: *How long, O Lord, dost Thou not judge and revenge our blood on them that dwell on the earth?* And in accordance with this we find them rejoicing in the vengeance taken upon sinners: *The just shall rejoice when he shall see the revenge.* It would seem, then, that we ought rather to pray against our enemies than for them.

But, on the contrary, as S. Augustine says: "The vengeance of the martyrs is the overthrow of the empire of sin under whose dominion they suffered so much"; or, as he says elsewhere: "They demand vengeance, not by word of mouth, but by very reason, just as the blood of Abel cried out from the earth." Moreover, they rejoice in this vengeance, not for its own sake, but because of the Divine Justice.

3. Lastly, a man's deeds and his prayers cannot be in opposition. But men sometimes quite lawfully attack their enemies, else all wars would be illegal. Hence we ought not to pray for our enemies.

But it is lawful to assail our enemies that so they may be hindered from sin; and this is for their good and for that of others. In the same way, then, it is lawful to pray for temporal evils for our enemies to the end that they may be corrected. In this sense our deeds and our prayers are not in opposition.

*S. Augustine:* If there were no wicked folk, then for whom could we be supposed to pray when we are told: *Pray for your enemies?* Perhaps you would like to have good enemies. Yet how could that be? For unless you yourself are bad you will not have good people for enemies; and if, on the contrary, you are good, then no one will be your enemy save the wicked folk (*Sermon*, xv., *on Ps.* xxv. 8).

"Have mercy upon us, O God of all, and behold us, and shew us the light of Thy mercies: And send Thy fear upon the nations, that have not sought after Thee: that they may know that there is no God beside Thee, and that they may shew forth Thy wonders. Lift up Thy hand over the strange nations, that they may see Thy power."

On the Seven Petitions of the *lord's Prayer*.

The Lord's Prayer is the most perfect of all prayers, for, as S. Augustine says to Proba: "If we pray rightly and fittingly we can say nothing else but what is set down in the *Lord's Prayer*." And since prayer is, in a sort, the interpreter of our desires before God, we can only rightly ask in prayer for those things which we can rightly desire. But in the *Lord's Prayer* not only do we have petitions for all those things which we can rightly desire, but they are set forth in the order in which they are to be desired. Hence this prayer not only teaches us how to pray, but serves as the norm of all our dispositions of mind.

For it is clear that we desire first the end and then the means to the attainment of that end. But our end is God, towards Whom our desires tend in two ways: first, in that we desire God's glory; secondly, in that we desire to enjoy that glory ourselves. The former of these pertains to that love wherewith we love God in Himself, the latter to that charity wherewith we love ourselves in God. Hence the first petition runs: *Hallowed be Thy Name*, wherein we pray for God's glory; and the second runs: *Thy kingdom come*, wherein we pray that we may come to the glory of His kingdom.

But to this said end things lead us in two ways: viz., either *essentially* or *accidentally*. Things which are useful for the attainment of that end *essentially* lead us to it. But a thing may be useful as regards that end which is the possession of God in two ways: namely, *directly and principally*, that is, according to the merits by which we merit the possession of God by obeying Him; and in accordance with this runs the petition: *Thy Will be done on earth as it is in Heaven*; also *instrumentally* as assisting us to merit, whence the petition: *Give us this day our daily bread*. And this is true whether we understand by this "bread" that Sacramental Bread, the daily use of Which profits man, and in Which are comprised all the other Sacraments; or whether we understand it of material bread so that "bread" here means all that is sufficient for the support of life—as S. Augustine explains it to Proba. For both the Holy Eucharist is the chief of Sacraments, and bread is the chief of foods, whence in the Gospel of S. Matthew we have the term "super-substantial" or "special" applied to it, as S. Jerome explains it.

And we are lead, as it were, *accidentally* to the possession of God by the removal of impediments from our path. Now there are three things which impede us in our efforts after the possession of God. The first of these is sin, which directly excludes us from the kingdom: *Neither fornicators, nor idolaters, ... etc., shall possess the kingdom of God*; hence the petition: *Forgive us our trespasses...*. And the second impediment is temptation which hinders us from obeying the Divine Will; whence the petition: *And lead us not into temptation*; in which petition we do not pray that we may not be tempted, but that we may not be overcome by temptation, for this is the meaning of being led into temptation. And the third hindrance lies in our present penal state which prevents us from having "the sufficiency of life"; and for this reason we say: *Deliver us from evil.*

Some, however, argue that these seven petitions are not very appropriate, thus:

1. It seems idle to pray that that may be hallowed which is already hallowed or holy. But the Name of God is holy: *And holy is His Name.* Similarly, His kingdom is everlasting: *Thy kingdom*, O Lord, *is a kingdom of all ages.* God's Will, too, is always fulfilled: *And all My Will shall be done.* Hence it is idle to pray that God's Name may be hallowed, that His kingdom may come, and that His Will may be done.

But, as S. Augustine says, when we say, *Hallowed be Thy Name*, we do not make this petition as though God's Name were not holy, but that It may be held holy by men; in other words, that God's glory may be propagated amongst men. And when we say, *Thy kingdom come*, it is not as though we meant that God did not reign, but, as S. Augustine says to Proba: "We stir up our desires for that kingdom, that it may come upon us and that we may reign in it." Lastly, when we say, *Thy Will be done*, this is rightly understood to mean: May Thy precepts be obeyed *on earth as in Heaven*—that is, as by Angels, so by men. These three petitions, then, will receive their perfect fulfilment in the life to come; but the remaining four, as S. Augustine says, refer to the necessities of the present life.

2. But further, to depart from evil must precede the pursuit of what is good. Hence it hardly seems appropriate to place those petitions which are concerned with the pursuit of what is good before those which refer to the departing from evil.

Yet since prayer is the interpreter of our desires the order of these petitions does not correspond to the order of attainment but of desire or intention; in this order, however, the end precedes the means to the end, the pursuit of good comes before the departure from evil.

3. But once more, we ask for something in order that it may be given us. But the chief gift of God is the Holy Spirit and those things which are given us through Him. Hence these petitions do not seem to be very appropriate since they do not correspond to the Gifts of the Holy Spirit.

S. Augustine, however, adapts these seven petitions to the Gifts of the Holy Spirit and to the Beatitudes; he says: "If we have the *fear of God* by which the poor in spirit are blessed, we pray that God's Name may be hallowed among men by chaste fear. If we have *piety*, by which the meek are blessed, we pray that His kingdom may come, that we may be meek, and that we may not withstand It. If we have *knowledge*, by which they that mourn are blessed, we pray that His will may be done, and that so we may not mourn. If we have *fortitude*, by which they that hunger are blessed, we pray that our daily bread may be given us. If we have *counsel*, by which they that are merciful are blessed, let us forgive our debtors that we ourselves may be forgiven. If we have *understanding*, by which the clean of heart are blessed, let us pray that we may not have a double heart that pursues after temporal things whence temptations come to us. If we have *wisdom*, whence the peace-makers are blessed—for they shall be called the sons of God—let us pray that we may be delivered from evil, for that very deliverance will make us the free sons of God."

4. Again, according to S. Luke, there are only five petitions in the Lord's Prayer. Hence it would seem superfluous to have seven in S. Matthew.

But, as S. Augustine says: "S. Luke only includes five petitions and not seven in the Lord's Prayer, for he shows that the third petition is, in a sense, only a repetition of the two preceding ones; by omitting it he makes us see that God's will is more especially concerned with our knowledge of His sanctity and with our reigning with Him. But Luke has omitted Matthew's last petition, *Deliver us from evil*, in order to show us that we are delivered from evil just precisely as we are not led into temptation."

5. And lastly, it seems idle to try to stir up the benevolence of one who is beforehand with his benevolence. But God does forestall us with His benevolence, for *He hath first loved us*. Consequently it seems superfluous to preface our petitions with the words *Our Father Who art in Heaven*, words which seem intended to stir up God's benevolence.

But we must remember that prayer is not directed to God in order to prevail upon Him, but in order to excite ourselves to confidence in our petitions. And this confidence is especially excited in us by consideration of His love towards us whereby He wishes us well, wherefore we say, *Our Father*, and of His pre-eminent power whereby He is able to assist us, whence we say, *Who art in Heaven*.

*Cajetan:* The first three petitions of the *Lord's Prayer* can also be referred to that which we principally desire, so that all three regard mainly that love wherewith we love God in Himself, and secondarily that love wherewith we love ourselves in God. And the proof of this is that in each of the first three we have the pronoun *Thine*, but in the last four the pronoun *our*. Thus the first petition asks for the effective and enduring praise of God's Name; the second, that He—and not the devil, nor the world, nor the flesh, nor sin—may reign effectively; the third, that His Will may be effectively fulfilled. For these things are not now absolutely so with God, and this by reason of the multitude of sins, and also because the mode of their present fulfilment is hidden. And the word *effectively* is introduced into each clause by reason of the subjoined qualification *on earth as it is in Heaven*, for this qualifies each of the foregoing clauses. Hence rightly do our desires first of all aim at, wish for, and pray that— even as something good for God Himself—He may be sanctified in His Name; that He may be permanently uplifted above all things—on earth as in Heaven; that He—not sin—may reign— on earth as in Heaven; that His Will—none other—may be done—on earth as in Heaven (*on* 2. 2. 83. 9).

*S. Augustine:* O Eternal Truth, True Love and lovable Eternity! Thou art my God; for Thee do I sigh night and day! And when I first knew Thee Thou didst snatch me up so that I saw that That really was Which I saw, and that I who saw was really not—as yet. And Thou didst beat back my weak gaze, pouring out Thy light upon me in its intensity; and I trembled with love and with horror. For I found myself to be far away from Thee in a land that was unlike Thee; it was as though I heard Thy Voice from on high, saying: "I am the Food of grown men, grow, and thou shalt eat Me, but thou shalt not be changed into Me" (*Confessions*, VII. x. 2).

*S. Augustine:* And the faithful are well aware of that Spiritual Food Which you, too, will soon know and Which you are to receive from God's altar. It will be your food, nay, your daily food, needful for this life. For are we not about to receive the Eucharist wherein we come to Christ Himself, and begin to reign with Him for ever? The Eucharist is our daily Bread. But let us so receive it as to be thereby refreshed, not in body merely but in mind. For the power which we know to be therein is the power of Unity whereby we are brought into union with His Body and become His members. Let us be What we receive; for then It will be truly our daily bread.

Again, what I set before you is your daily bread; and what you hear read day by day in the church is your daily bread; and the hymns you hear and which you sing—they are your daily bread. For these things we need for our pilgrimage. But when we get There are we going to hear a book read? Nay, we are going to hear the Word Himself; we are going to see the Word Himself; we are going to eat Him, to drink Him, even as the Angels do already. Do the Angels need books, or disputations, or readers? Nay, not so. But by seeing they read, for they see the Truth Itself and are sated from that Fount whence we receive but the sprinkling of the dew (*Sermon*, lvii., *on S. Matt.* vi. 7).

*S. Augustine:* When ye say *Give us this day our daily bread*, ye profess yourselves God's beggars. Yet blush not at it! The richest man on earth is God's beggar. The beggar stands at the rich man's door. But the rich man in his turn stands at the door of one richer than he. He is begged from, and he, too, has to beg. If he were not in need he would not beseech God in prayer. But what can the rich man need? I dare to say it: he needs even his daily bread! For how is it that he abounds with all things, save that God gave them to him? And what will they have if God but withdraw His hand? (*Sermon*, lvi. 9, *on S. Matt.* vi.).

*S. Augustine:* Think not that you have no need to say *Forgive us our trespasses as we forgive them that trespass against us....* He who looks with pleasure at what he should not—sins. Yet who can control the glance of the eye? Indeed, some say that the eye is so called from its swiftness (*oculus a velocitate*). Who can control his eyes or his ears? You can close your eyes when you like, but how quickly they open again! You can shut your ears with an effort; put up your hand, and you can touch them. But if someone holds your hands your ears remain open, and you cannot then shut out cursing words, impure words, flattering and deceitful words. When you hear something which you should not—do you not sin with your ears? What when you hear some evil thing with pleasure? And the death-dealing tongue! How many sins it commits! (*Sermon*, lvi. 8).

*S. Augustine:* Indeed, our whole righteousness—true righteousness though it be, by reason of the True Good to Whom it is referred, consists rather, as long as we are in this life, in the remission of our sins than in the perfection of our virtues. And the proof of this is the Prayer of the whole City of God which is in pilgrimage on this earth. For by all Its members It cries to God: *Forgive us our trespasses as we forgive them the trespass against us!* And this Prayer is of no avail for those whose faith is without works—dead; but only for those whose faith worketh through charity. For though our reason is indeed subject to God, yet in this our mortal condition, in this corruptible body which weigheth down the soul, our reason does not perfectly control our vices, and hence such prayer as this is needful for the righteous (*Of the City of God*, xix. 27).

"Father, the hour is come; glorify Thy Son, that Thy Son may glorify Thee. As Thou hast given Him power over all flesh, that He may give life everlasting to all whom Thou hast given Him. And this is life everlasting, that they may know Thee, the only true God, and Jesus Christ, Whom Thou hast sent."

Rhythm in Honour of the Blessed Sacrament, said to have been composed by S. Thomas on his Death-Bed.

Adoro Te devote, latens Deitas,Quæ sub his figuris vere latitas;Tibi se cor meum totum subjicit,Quia Te contemplans totum deficit.

Visus, tactus gustus, in Te fallitur,Sed auditu solo tuto creditur;Credo quidquid dixit Dei Filius,Nil hoc verbo veritatis verius.

In cruce latebat sola Deitas,At hic latet simul et humanitas;Ambo tamen credens atque confitens,Peto quod petivit latro poenitens.

Plagas, sicut Thomas, non intueor,Deum tamen meum Te confiteor;Fac me Tibi semper magis credere,In Te spem habere, Te diligere.

O memoriale mortis Domini,Panis vivus, vitam præstans homini,Præsta meæ menti de Te vivero,Et Te illi semper dulce sapere.

Pie Pellicane Jesu Domine,Me immundum munda Tuo Sanguine,Cujus una stilla salvum facereTotum mundum quit ab omni scelere.

Jesu Quem velatum nunc aspicio,Oro fiat illud quod tam sitio,Ut Te revelata cernens facie,Visu sim beatus Tuæ gloriæ!

(An Indulgence of 100 days for the recitation of this rhythm. *S. Congr. of Indulgences*, December 20, 1884.)

X

Is Prayer Peculiar to Rational Creatures?

Prayer is an act of the reason, as we have shown above. And rational creatures are so termed because of the possession of reason. Consequently prayer is peculiar to them.

As we have said above, prayer is an act of the reason by which a person pleads with his superior, just in the same way as a command is an act of the reason by which an inferior is directed to do something. Prayer, then, properly pertains to one who has the use of reason and who also has a superior with whom he can plead. The Persons of the Trinity have no superior; the brute animals have no reason. Hence prayer belongs neither to the Divine Persons nor to the brute creation, but is peculiar to rational creatures.

Some, however, argue that prayer cannot be peculiar to rational creatures, thus:

1. To ask and to receive belong to the same person. But the Divine Persons receive: the Son, namely, and the Holy Spirit. Consequently They can also pray; indeed it is the Son Himself Who says, *I will ask the Father*, and the Apostle says of the Holy Spirit, *The Spirit Himself asketh for us*.

But it belongs to the Divine Persons to receive by Their nature, whereas to pray belongs to one who receives through grace. The Son is said to ask or pray according to the nature He took upon Himself—that is according to His Human, and not according to His Divine, Nature; the Holy Spirit, too, is said to petition because He makes us petition.

2. But further, the Angels are superior to the rational creation since they are intellectual substances; but it belongs to the Angels to pray, for it is said in the Psalm: *Adore Him, all ye His Angels*.

But the intellect and the reason are not different faculties in us, though they do differ in the sense that one is more perfect than the other. Consequently the intellectual creation, such as are the Angels, is sometimes distinguished from the rational creation, but at other times both are embraced under the one term "rational." And it is in this latter sense of the term "rational" that prayer is said to be peculiar to the rational creation.

3. Lastly, he prays who calls upon God; for it is chiefly by prayer that we call upon God. But the brute animals also call upon God, for the Psalmist says: *Who giveth to beasts their food, and to the young ravens that call upon Him*.

But the young ravens are said to call upon God by reason of those natural desires by which all things, each in their own fashion, desire to obtain the Divine goodness. In the same way brute animals are said to obey God by reason of the natural instinct by which they are moved by God.

"Reward them that patiently wait for Thee, that Thy Prophets may be found faithful: and hear the prayers of Thy servants. According to the blessing of Aaron over Thy people, and direct us into the way of justice, and let all know that dwell upon the earth, that Thou art God the beholder of all ages."

XI

Do the Saints in Heaven Pray for Us?

*This is he who prayeth much for the people and for all the holy city, Jeremias the Prophet of God.*

As S. Jerome says, Vigilantius's error lay in maintaining that "while we live we can mutually pray for one another; but after we are dead no one's prayer for another is heard, and this is especially clear in the case of the Martyrs who were unable to obtain by their prayers vengeance for their blood."

But this is altogether false; for since prayer for others springs from charity, the more perfect the charity of those who are in Heaven the more they pray for those wayfarers on earth who can be helped by their prayers. And the more knit they are to God the more efficacious are their prayers; for the Divine harmony demands that the superabundance of those who are in the higher position should redound upon those who are lower, just as the brightness of the sun renders the atmosphere itself luminous. Whence Christ Himself is said to be *Approaching of Himself to God to intercede for us.* Whence, too, S. Jerome's reply to Vigilantius: "If the Apostles and Martyrs, when they were still in the body, and had still to be solicitous on their own account, prayed for others, how much more when they have won the crown, when they have gained the victory and the triumph?"

Yet some maintain that the Blessed in Heaven do not pray for us, thus:

1. A man's acts are more meritorious for himself than for another. But the Saints who are in Heaven neither merit for themselves nor pray for themselves, for they have already attained the goal of their desires. Hence neither do they pray for us.

But the Saints who are in our Fatherland lack no Blessedness—since they are Blessed—save the glory of the body, and for this they pray. But they pray for us who still lack the ultimate perfection of Blessedness; and their prayers are efficacious by reason of their previous merits and of the Divine acceptation of their prayers.

2. But once more: the Saints are perfectly conformed to the Will of God, and consequently will nothing but what He wills. But what God wills is always fulfilled. Hence it is idle for the Saints to pray for us.

But the Saints obtain that which God wills should come about through the medium of their prayers; and they ask for what they think is, by God's Will, to be fulfilled through their prayers.

3. And yet again: just as the Saints in Heaven are superior to us so also are they who are in Purgatory—for they cannot sin. Those, however, who are in Purgatory do not pray for us, but rather we for them. It follows, then, that neither can the Saints in Heaven pray for us.

But though those who are in Purgatory are superior to us in that they cannot sin, yet are they our inferiors as regards the penalties they suffer; hence they are not in a state to pray for us, but rather we for them.

4. Once more: if the Saints in Heaven could pray for us it would follow that the prayers of the holiest Saints would be the most efficacious, and that consequently we ought not to ask the inferior Saints to pray for us, but only the greatest ones.

But God desires inferior things to be helped by all that are superior, and consequently we have to implore the aid of not only the chief Saints but also of the lesser; else it would follow that we ought to implore mercy from God alone. And it may sometimes happen that the petition made to a lesser Saint is more efficacious, either because we ask him more devoutly, or because God wishes thus to show forth his sanctity.

5. Lastly, Peter's soul is not Peter. Consequently if the souls of the Saints could pray for us, we ought—as long as their souls are separated from their bodies—to appeal, not to Peter to help us, but to Peter's soul; whereas the Church does the contrary. From which it would seem that the Saints, at all events previous to the Resurrection, do not pray for us.

But since the Saints merited when alive that they should pray for us, we therefore call upon them by the names they bore when here below, and by which they are best known to us; and we do this, too, in order to show our faith in the Resurrection, in accordance with the words *I am the God of Abraham*.

*Cajetan:* The question arises: how could Jeremias, who in the days of the Maccabees was not yet in our Fatherland but still in the Limbo of the Fathers, pray for Jerusalem?

But if we carefully consider what it is at root which makes the prayers of the Saints in the Fatherland avail for us, we shall find that the same reason holds for the Saints who were in Limbo as for those who enjoy the Beatific Vision. For it is their charity in their state of absolute superiority to us which is the reason for their praying for us. Hence, in the reply to the third difficulty, those who are in Purgatory are excluded from the number of those who pray for us because they are not altogether our superiors, but by reason of their sufferings are inferior to us, and need our prayers.

But the Fathers in Limbo were, it is clear, confirmed in charity and were incapable of sin, neither were they liable to any peculiar or fresh suffering. For while the pain of loss was common to them and to the sojourners on earth, the former were free from all pain of sense, hence they could pray for us. There is, however, this difference to be noted between them and the Saints in the Fatherland—viz., that whereas the former had it in common with the latter to pray for those sojourning on earth, it is given only to the Saints in the Fatherland to see the prayers of us sojourners addressed to them. Hence Jeremias is here said to pray, he is not said to have heard their prayers or supplications (*on* 2. 2. 83. 11).

XII

Should Prayer be Vocal?

*I cried to the Lord with my voice, with my voice I made supplication to the Lord.*

Prayer is of two kinds: public and private. *Public* or common prayer is that which is offered to God by the Church's ministers in the person of the whole body of the faithful. And it is necessary that such prayer should be known to the body of the faithful for whom it is offered; this, however, could not be unless it were vocal; consequently it is reasonably enacted that the Church's ministers should pronounce such prayers in a loud voice so as to reach the ears of all.

*Private* prayer, on the contrary, is that which is offered by private individuals, whether for themselves or for others; and its nature does not demand that it should be vocal. At the same time, we can use our voices in this kind of prayer, and this for three reasons: Firstly, in order to excite interior devotion whereby our minds may, when we pray, be lifted up to God; for men's minds are moved by external signs—whether words or acts—to understand, and, by consequence, also to feel. Wherefore S. Augustine says to Proba: "By words and other signs we vehemently stir ourselves up so as to increase our holy desires." Hence in private prayer we must make such use of words and other signs as shall avail to rouse our minds interiorly. But if, on the other hand, such things only serve to distract the mind, or prove in any way a hindrance, then we must cease from them; this is especially the case with those whose minds are sufficiently prepared for devotion without such incentives. Thus the Psalmist says: *My heart hath said to Thee, My face hath sought Thee;* and of Anna we are told that *she spoke within her heart.*

And secondly, we make use of vocal prayer in payment, as it were, of a just debt—in order, that is, to serve God with the entirety of what we have received from Him; consequently not with our mind alone but with our body as well; and this, as the Prophet Osee says, is especially suitable to prayer considered as a satisfaction for our sins: *Take away all iniquity and receive the good, and we will render the calves of our lips.*

And thirdly, we sometimes make use of vocal prayer because the soul overflows, as it were, on to the body by reason of the vehemence of our feelings, as it is written: *My heart hath been glad, and my tongue hath rejoiced.*

But it seems to some that prayer should not be vocal, thus:

1. Prayer is, as we have said, principally directed to God, and God knows the heart's speech. Consequently to add vocal prayer is idle.

But vocal prayer is not employed in order to manifest to God something which He did not know, but to stir up the mind of him who prays, and of others, too, towards God.

2. Again, man's mind is meant to rise by prayer towards God; but words, and other things pertaining to the senses, keep back a man from the ascent of contemplation.

Words appertaining to other things than God do indeed distract the mind and hinder the devotion of him who prays; but devotional words stir up the mind, especially if it be less devout.

3. Lastly, prayer ought to be offered to God in secret, according to the words: *But thou when thou shalt pray, enter into thy chamber, and having shut the door, pray to thy Father in secret*; whereas to pray vocally means to publish it abroad.

But, as S. Chrysostom says: "The Lord forbade us to pray in public with a view to being seen by the public. Consequently, when we pray we should do nothing novel to attract men's attention, whether by uttering cries which may be heard by them, or by openly beating our breasts, or by spreading out our hands, for the crowd to see us." While, on the other hand, as S. Augustine remarks: "To be seen by men is not wrong, but to do things to be seen by men."

*Cajetan:* Note carefully, ye who murmur at the Church's services, these three points: the different kinds of vocal prayer, its necessity, and the conditions attaching to it. For vocal prayer is divided into that which is in common and that which is private or individual.

The general necessity of vocal prayer arises from the fact that it is offered in the person of the Church. For since the Church is composed of created beings dependent on the senses, prayer made through the medium of the senses—*i.e.*, vocal prayer—must needs be offered by its ministers; else we should not know whether the worship of prayer was being offered by God's ministers, nor should we be conscious of the gift to God which was being offered by them in prayer; for the Church only judges from the things that appear externally.

Our individual need of vocal prayer arises from the necessity of stirring up our own devotion, and preserving it.

The conditions of prayer in common are twofold: it must be vocal, and it must be out loud. Hence those who say private Masses in such a low tone—and that consciously—as to be unintelligible to their hearers, appear to act unreasonably and are inexcusable, unless it should happen by accident that no one is present; in this case it is sufficient if they can be heard by the server who is close at hand. This will also show us what use we are to make of chant, or of recitation without chant, in prayer in common: it must be governed by our common devotion. And in whatever fashion such prayer may be made this rule must always be observed: it must be said so intelligibly that the meaning of the words may be distinctly perceived both by the reciters and by others, that so the Church's devotion may be aroused.

And reason tells us what conditions attach to our private prayer: viz., our own private devotion. This shews, too, the error of those who, in order to complete the tale of a large number of private vocal prayers each day, lay aside meditation and mental prayer. They neglect the end for the means (*on* 2. 2. 83. 12).

*S. Augustine:* Oh! How I lifted up my voice to Thee, O Lord, when I sang the Psalms of David, those songs full of faith, those strains full of piety which soothed my swelling spirit! And I was then but uninstructed in Thy true love; a catechumen spending my leisure with Alypius, another catechumen. And my mother stayed with us: clad indeed in woman's garb, but with a man's faith, with a matron's calm, with a mother's love, with a Christian's piety. Oh! How I lifted up my voice in those Psalms! How they inflamed my heart! How I yearned to recite them, if I could, to the whole world—as an answer to the pride of the human race! Though, indeed, they are sung throughout the world, and none can hide himself from Thy heat! (*Confess.*, IX. iv. 8).

*S. Augustine:* Sometimes, indeed, through immoderate fear of this mistake I err by excessive severity; nay, sometimes, though it is but rarely, I could almost wish to shut out from my ears and even from the Church itself all those sweet-sounding melodies used in the accompaniment of David's Psalms. Sometimes it seems to me as though it would be safer to do as I have often heard that Athanasius, the Bishop of Alexandria, did, for he made the reader of the Psalms so modulate his voice that he came to be rather speaking than singing. Yet, on the other hand, when I remember the tears which I shed when I heard the Church's chant in the early days of my regaining the faith, and when I notice that even now I am stirred—not so much by the chant as by the things that are chanted—when, that is, they are chanted with clear intonation and suitable modulation, then once more I recognize the great value of this appointed fashion (*Confess.*, X. xxxiii. 50).

*S. Augustine: I have cried with my whole heart, hear me, O Lord!* Who can question but that when men pray their cry to the Lord is vain if it be nought but the sound of the corporeal voice and their heart be not intent upon God? But if their prayer come from the heart, then, even though the voice of the body be silent, it may be hidden from all men, yet not from God. Whether, then, we pray to God with our voice—at times when such prayer is necessary—or whether we pray in silence, it is our heart that must send forth the cry. But the heart's cry is the earnest application of our minds. And when this accompanies our prayer it expresses the deep affections of him who yearns and asks and so despairs not of his request. And further, a man cries *with his whole heart* when he has no other thought. Such prayers with many are rare; with few are they frequent; I know not whether anyone's prayers are always so (*Enarr. in Ps.* cxviii., *Sermon*, xxix. 1).

"Incline Thy ear, O Lord, and hear me; for I am needy and poor. Preserve my soul, for I am holy: save Thy servant, O my God, that trusteth in Thee. Have mercy on me, O Lord, for I have cried to Thee all the day. Give joy to the soul of Thy servant, for to Thee, O Lord, I have lifted up my soul. For Thou, O Lord, art sweet and mild; and plenteous in mercy to all that call upon Thee."

XIII

Must Prayer necessarily be Attentive?

That even holy men sometimes suffer distraction of mind when at prayer is clear from the words: *My heart hath forsaken me!*

This question particularly concerns vocal prayer. And for its solution we must know that a thing is said to be necessary in two senses: firstly, in the sense that by it a certain end is *more readily* attained, and in this sense attention is absolutely requisite in prayer. But a thing is said to be necessary also because without it a certain thing cannot attain its object *at all*. Now the effect or object of prayer is threefold. Its first effect—an effect, indeed, which is common to all acts springing from charity—is *merit*; but to secure this effect it is not necessarily required that attention should be kept up throughout the prayer, but the initial intention with which a man comes to prayer renders the whole prayer meritorious, as, indeed, is the case in all other meritorious acts.

The second effect of prayer is peculiar to it, and that is to *obtain favours*; and for this, too, the primary intention suffices, and to it God principally looks. But if the primary intention is wanting, prayer is not meritorious, neither can it win favours; for, as S. Gregory says, God hears not the prayer of a man who when he prays does not give heed to God.

The third effect of prayer is that which it immediately and actually brings about, namely, the *spiritual refreshment of the soul*; and to attain this end attention is necessarily required in prayer. Whence it is said, *If I pray in a tongue my understanding is without fruit.*

At the same time, we must remember that there is a threefold species of attention which may find place in our vocal prayer: one by which a man attends to the words he recites, and is careful to make no mistake in them; another by which he attends to the meaning of the words; and a third by which he attends to the end of all prayer—namely, God Himself—and to the object for which he is praying. And this species of attention is the most necessary of all, and one which even uninstructed folk can have; sometimes, indeed, the intensity with which the mind is borne towards God is, as says Hugh of S. Victor, so overwhelming that the mind is oblivious of all else.

Some, however, argue that prayer must of necessity be attentive, thus:

I. It is said in S. John's Gospel: *God is a spirit, and they that adore Him must adore Him in spirit and truth*. But inattentive prayer is not *in spirit*.

But he prays *in spirit and in truth* who comes to pray moved by the impulse of the Spirit, even though, owing to human infirmity, his mind afterwards wanders.

2. But again, prayer is "the ascent of the mind towards God." But when prayer is inattentive the mind does not ascend towards God.

But the human mind cannot, owing to Nature's weakness, long remain on high, for the soul is dragged down to lower things by the weight of human infirmity; and hence it happens that when the mind of one who prays ascends towards God in contemplation it suddenly wanders away from Him owing to his infirmity.

3. Lastly, prayer must needs be without sin. But not without sin does a man suffer distraction of mind when he prays, for he seems to mock God, just as if one were to speak with his fellow-man and not attend to what he said. Consequently S. Basil says: "The Divine assistance is to be implored, not remissly, nor with a mind that wanders here and there; for such a one not only will not obtain what he asks, but will rather be mocking God."

Of course, if a man purposely allowed his mind to wander in prayer, he would commit a sin and hinder the fruit of his prayer. Against such S. Augustine says in his *Rule*: "When you pray to God in Psalms and hymns, entertain your heart with what your lips are reciting." But that distraction of mind which is unintentional does not destroy the fruit of prayer.

Hence S. Basil also says: "But if through the weakness of sinful nature you cannot pray with attention, restrain your imagination as far as you can, and God will pardon you, inasmuch as it is not from negligence but from weakness that you are unable to occupy yourself with Him as you should."

*Cajetan:* Does a man satisfy the precept of the Church if, being bound to the recitation of the Divine Office, he sets out with the intention of meditating upon the Divine Goodness or upon the Passion of Christ, and thus keeping his mind firmly fixed upon God? Clearly a man who strives to keep his mind occupied during the whole of the Divine Office with contemplation of and devout affections towards God and Divine things fully satisfies his obligation. So, too, a man who aims at meditation on the Passion of Christ and devout affections on it during the whole Office, undoubtedly satisfies his obligation, for he is making use of a better means for keeping in touch with the Divinity than if he merely dwelt upon the meaning of the words. At the same time, he must be ready to lay this aside if in the course of the Office he finds himself uplifted to Divine things, for at this he must primarily aim. One who so prays, then, must make the Passion of Christ a means and not an end; he must, that is, be prepared to ascend thereby, if God grants it, to Divine things. In short, we may make use of any one of the species of attention enumerated above provided we do not exclude the higher forms. Thus, for example, if a man feels that it is more suited to his small capacity to aim simply at making no mistakes, and habitually makes use of this form of attention, he must still use it as a means only; he must, that is, be at God's disposition, for God may have mercy upon him and grant him, by reason of his dispositions, some better form of attention.

Again, when a person prays for things needful for his support in life he must not be so occupied with the thought of these things as to appear to subordinate Divine things to human, as though prayer was but a means and his daily living the end. We must bear in mind the doctrine laid down above—viz., that *all our prayers should tend to the attainment of grace and glory.* We must occupy ourselves with the thought of eternal glory, or of the glory of the adoption of sons during this life, or with the virtues as means to arriving at our eternal home, and as the adornment of the inhabitants of heaven, and the commencement here of heavenly "conversation"; such things as these must be counted as the highest forms of attention (*on* 2. 2. 83. 13).

*S. Augustine: Give joy to the soul of Thy servant, for to Thee, O Lord, I have lifted up my soul. For Thou, O Lord, art sweet and mild.* It seems to me that he calls God "mild" because He endures all our vagaries, and only awaits our prayers that He may perfect us. And when we offer Him our prayers He accepts them gratefully and hears them. Neither does He reflect on the careless way in which we pour them out, He even accepts prayers of which we are hardly conscious! For, Brethren, what man is there who would put up with it if a friend of his began a conversation with him, and yet, just when he was ready to reply to what his friend said, should discover that he was paying no attention to him but was saying something to someone else? Or supposing you were to appeal to a judge and were to appoint a place for him to hear your appeal, and then suddenly, while you were talking with him, were to put him aside and begin to gossip with a friend! How long would he put up with you? And yet God puts up with the hearts of so many who pray to Him and who yet are thinking of other things, even evil things, even wicked things, things hateful to God; for even to think of unnecessary things is an insult to Him with Whom you have begun to talk. For your prayer is a conversation with God. When you read, God speaks to you; when you pray, you speak to God.... And you may picture God saying to you: "You forget how often you have stood before Me and have thought of such idle and superfluous things and have so rarely poured out to Me an attentive and definite prayer!" But *Thou, O Lord, art sweet and mild!* Thou art sweet, bearing with me! It is from weakness that I slip away! Heal me and I shall stand; strengthen me and I shall be firm! But until Thou dost so, bear with me, for *Thou, O Lord, art sweet and mild* (*Enarr. in Ps.* lxxxv. 7).

*S. Augustine: Praise the Lord, O my soul!* What mean these words, Brethren? Do we not praise the Lord? Do we not sing hymns day by day? Do not our mouths, each according to their measure, sound forth day by day the praises of God? And what is it we praise? It is a great Thing that we praise, but that wherewith we praise is weak as yet. When does the singer fill up the praises of Him Whom he sings? A man stands and sings before God, often for a long space; but oftentimes, whilst his lips move to frame the words of his song, his thoughts fly away to I know not what desires! And so, too, our mind has sometimes been fixed on praising God in a definite manner, but our soul has flitted away, led hither and thither by divers desires and anxious cares. And then our mind, as though from up above, has looked down upon the soul as it flitted to and fro, and has seemed to turn to it and address its uneasy wanderings—saying to it: *Praise the Lord, O my soul!* Why art thou anxious about other things than Him? Why busy thyself with the mortal things of earth? And then our soul, as though weighed down and unable to stand firm as it should, replies to our mind: *I will praise the Lord in my life!* Why does it say *in my life*? Why? Because now I am in my death!

Rouse yourself, then, and say: *Praise the Lord, O my soul!* And your soul will reply to you: "I praise Him as much as I can, though it is but weakly, in small measure, and with little strength." But why so? Because *while we are in the body we are absent from the Lord*. And why do you thus praise the Lord so imperfectly and with so little fixity of attention? Ask Holy Scripture: *The corruptible body weigheth down the soul, and the earthly habitation presseth down the mind that museth upon many things.* O take away, then, my body which weigheth down the soul, and then will I praise the Lord! Take away my earthly habitation which presseth down the mind that museth upon many things, so that, instead of many things I may be occupied with One Thing alone, and may praise the Lord! But as long as I am as I am, I cannot, for I am weighed down! What then? Wilt thou be silent? Wilt thou never perfectly praise the Lord? *I will praise the Lord in my life!* (*Enarr in Ps.* cxlv. 1).

"My spirit is in anguish within me; my heart within me is troubled. I remembered the days of old, I meditated on all Thy works; I meditated upon the works of Thy hands. I stretched forth my hands to Thee; my soul is as earth without water unto Thee. Hear me speedily, O Lord: my spirit hath fainted away."

*S. Thomas:* The fruits of prayer are twofold. For first there is the merit which thereby accrues to a man; and, secondly, there is the spiritual consolation and devotion which is begotten of prayer. And he who does not attend to, or does not understand his prayer, loses that fruit which is spiritual consolation; but we cannot say that he loses that fruit which is merit, for then we should have to say that very many prayers were without merit since a man can hardly say the *Lord's Prayer* without some distraction of mind. Hence we must rather say that when a person is praying and is sometimes distracted from what he is saying, or—more generally—when a person is occupied with some meritorious work and does not continuously and at every moment reflect that he is doing it for God, his work does not cease to be meritorious. And the reason is that in meritorious acts directed to a right end it is not requisite that our intention should be referred to that end at every moment, but the influence of the intention with which we begun persists throughout even though we now and again be distracted in some particular point; and the influence of this initial intention renders the whole body of what we do meritorious unless it be broken off by reason of some contrary affection intruding itself and diverting us from the end we had first in view to some other end contrary to it.

And it must be remembered that there are three kinds of attention. The first is attention to the words we are actually saying; and sometimes this is harmful, for it may hinder devotion. The second is attention to the meaning of the words, and this, too, may be harmful, though not gravely so. The third is attention to the goal of our prayer, and this better and almost necessary (*Commentary on 1 Cor.* xiv. 14).

XIV

Should our Prayers be Long?

It would seem that we ought to pray continuously, for our Lord said: *We ought always to pray and not to faint;* so also S. Paul: *Pray without ceasing.*

But we must notice that when we speak of prayer we can mean either prayer *considered in itself* or the *cause of prayer.* Now the *cause of prayer* is the desire of the love of God; and all prayer ought to spring from this desire which is, indeed, continuous in us, whether actually or virtually, since this desire virtually remains in everything which we do from charity. But we ought to do all things for the glory of God: *whether you eat or whether you drink, or whatsoever else you do, do all to the glory of God.* In this sense, then, prayer ought to be continual. Hence S. Augustine says to Proba: "Therefore by our faith, by our hope, and by our charity, we are always praying, for our desire is continued."

But *prayer considered in itself* cannot be so continuous; for we must needs be occupied with other things. Hence S. Augustine says in the same place: "At certain intervals, at divers hours and times, we pray to God in words so that by these outward signs of things we may admonish ourselves, and may learn what progress we have made in this same desire, and may stir ourselves up to increase it."

But the quantity of a thing has to be determined by its purpose, just as a draught has to be proportioned to the health of the man who takes it. Consequently it is fitting that prayer should only last so long as it avails to stir up in us this fervour of interior desire. And when it exceeds this measure, and its prolongation only results in weariness, it must not be prolonged further. Hence S. Augustine also says to Proba: "The Brethren in Egypt are said to have had frequent prayers; but they were exceedingly brief, hardly more than eager ejaculations; and they adopted this method lest, if they prolonged their prayer, that vigilant attention which is requisite for prayer should lose its keen edge and become dulled. And thus they clearly show that this same attention, just as it is not to be forced if it fails to last, so neither is it to be quickly broken off if it does last."

And just as we have to pay attention to this in our private prayers, and have to be guided by our powers of attention, so must we observe the same principles in public prayer where we have to be governed by the people's devotion.

Some, however, argue that our prayers ought not to be continual, thus:

1. Our Lord said: *And when you are praying speak not much.* But it is not easy to see how a man can pray long without "speaking much"; more especially if it is a question of vocal prayer.

But S. Augustine says to Proba: "To prolong our prayer does not involve 'much-speaking.' 'Much-speaking' is one thing; the unceasing desire of the heart is another. Indeed we are told of the Lord Himself that *He passed the whole night in the prayer of God*; and, again, that *being in an agony He prayed the longer*, and this that He might afford us an example." And Augustine adds a little later: "Much speaking in prayer is to be avoided, but not much petition, if fervent attention lasts. For 'much-speaking' in prayer means the use of superfluous words when we pray for something necessary; but much petition means that with unceasing and devout stirrings of the heart we knock at His door to Whom we pray; and this is often a matter rather of groans than of words, of weeping than of speaking."

2. Further, prayer is but the unfolding of our desires. But our desires are holy in proportion as they are confined to one thing, in accordance with those words of the Psalmist: *One thing I have asked of the Lord, this will I seek after.* Whence it would seem to follow that our prayers are acceptable to God just in proportion to their brevity. But to prolong our prayer does not mean that we ask for many things, but that our hearts are continuously set upon one object for which we yearn.

3. Once more, it is unlawful for a man to transgress the limits which God Himself has fixed, especially in matters which touch the Divine worship, according to the words: *Charge the people lest they should have a mind to pass the limits to see the Lord, and a very great multitude of them should perish.* But God Himself has assigned limits to our prayer by instituting the *Lord's Prayer*, as is evident from the words: *Thus shalt thou pray.* Hence we ought not to extend our prayer beyond these limits. But our Lord did not institute this prayer with a view to tying us down exclusively to these words when we pray, but to show us that the scope of our prayer should be limited to asking only for the things contained in it, whatever form of words we may use or whatever may be our thoughts.

4. And lastly, with regard to the words of our Lord *that we ought always to pray and not to faint*, and those of S. Paul, *Pray without ceasing*, we must remark that a man prays without ceasing, either because of the unceasing nature of his desire, as we have above explained; or because he does not fail to pray at the appointed times; or because of the effect which his prayer has, whether upon himself—since even when he has finished praying he still remains devout—or upon others, as, for instance, when a man by some kind action induces another to pray for him whereas he himself desists from his prayer.

"Our soul waiteth for the Lord; for He is our helper and protector. For in Him our hearts shall rejoice; and in His Holy Name we have trusted. Let Thy mercy, O Lord, be upon us, as we have hoped in Thee."

XV

Is Prayer Meritorious?

On the words of the Psalmist, *My prayer shall be turned into my bosom*, the interlinear Gloss has: "And if it is of no profit to them (for whom it is offered), at least I myself shall not lose my reward." A reward, however, can only be due to merit. Prayer, then, is meritorious.

As we have said above, prayer has, besides the effect of spiritual consolation which it brings with it, a twofold power regarding the future: the power, namely, of meriting, and that of winning favours. But prayer, as indeed every other virtuous act, derives its power of meriting from that root which is charity, and the true and proper object of charity is that Eternal Good, the enjoyment of Which we merit. Now prayer proceeds from charity by means of the virtue of religion whose proper act is prayer; there accompany it, however, certain other virtues which are requisite for a good prayer—namely, faith and humility. For it belongs to the virtue of religion to offer our prayers to God; while to charity belongs the desire of that the attainment of which we seek in prayer. And faith is necessary as regards God to Whom we pray; for we must, of course, believe that from Him we can obtain what we ask. Humility, too, is called for on the part of the petitioner, for he must acknowledge his own needs. And devotion also is necessary; though this comes under religion of which it is the first act, it conditions all subsequent effects.

And its power of obtaining favours prayer owes to the grace of God to Whom we pray, and Who, indeed, induces us to pray. Hence S. Augustine says: "He would not urge us to ask unless He were ready to give"; and S. Chrysostom says: "He never refuses His mercies to them who pray, since it is He Who in His loving-kindness stirs them up so that they weary not in prayer."

But some say that prayer cannot be meritorious, thus:

1. Merit proceeds from grace, but prayer precedes grace, since it is precisely by prayer that we win grace: *Your Father from Heaven will give the Good Spirit to them that ask Him.*

But prayer, like any other virtuous act, cannot be meritorious without that grace which makes us pleasing to God. Yet even that prayer which wins for us the grace which renders us pleasing to God must proceed from some grace—that is, from some gratuitous gift; for, as S. Augustine says, to pray at all is a gift of God.

2. Again, prayer cannot be meritorious, for if it were so it would seem natural that prayer should especially merit that for which we actually pray. Yet this is not always the case, for even the prayers of the Saints are often not heard; S. Paul, for example, was not heard when he prayed that the sting of the flesh might be taken away from him.

But we must notice that the merit of our prayers sometimes lies in something quite different from what we beg for. For whereas merit is to be especially referred to the possession of God, our petitions in our prayers at times refer directly to other things, as we have pointed out above. Consequently, if what a man asks for will not tend to his ultimate attainment of God, he does not merit it by his prayer; sometimes, indeed, by asking and desiring such a thing he may lose all merit, as, for example, if a man were to ask of God something which was sinful and which he could not reverently ask for. Sometimes, however, what he asks for is not necessary for his salvation, nor yet is it clearly opposed to his salvation; and when a man so

6. Owing to the powerful and destructive nature of tornadoes, there are, perhaps not surprisingly, a number of myths and misconceptions surrounding them. For instance, many people mistakenly believe that tornadoes never occur over rivers, lakes, and oceans; yet, waterspouts, tornadoes that form over bodies of water, often move onshore and cause extensive damage to coastal areas. In addition, tornadoes can accompany hurricanes and tropical storms as they move to land. Another common myth about tornadoes is that damage to built structures, like houses and office buildings, can be avoided if windows are opened prior to the impact of the storm.

What can be inferred about the public's knowledge of tornadoes?
A.     A large number of people know how to avoid tornado damage.
B.     Most people appreciate the risk of death associated with tornadoes.
C.     Some members of the public know how to regulate the pressure inside buildings.
D.     Many people are not fully aware of certain key information about tornadoes.


7. Born in France in 1896, Jean Piaget was one of the most influential thinkers in the area of child development in the twentieth century. Piaget posited that children go through a stage of assimilation as they grow to maturity. Assimilation refers to the process of transforming one's environment in order to bring about its conformance to innate cognitive schemes and structures. Schemes used in infant breast feeding and bottle feeding are examples of assimilation because the child utilizes his or her innate capacity for sucking to complete both tasks.

Why does the writer mention bottle feeding in the above paragraph?
A.     To identify one of the important features of assimilation.
B.     To exemplify the assimilation process.
C.     To describe the importance of assimilation.
D.     To explain difficulties children face during assimilation.


8. Inherent social and cultural biases pervaded the manner in which archeological findings were investigated during the early nineteenth century because little attention was paid to the roles that wealth, status, and nationality played in the recovery and interpretation of artifacts. However, in the 1860s Charles Darwin established the theory that human beings are the ultimate product of a long biological evolutionary process. Darwinian theory infiltrated the discipline of archeology and heavily influenced the manner in which archeological artifacts were recovered and analyzed. As a result of Darwinism, there was a surge in artifacts excavated from African and Asian localities by the late 1900s.

Based on the information in the passage, what can be inferred about the early 1900s?
A.    There were few archeological findings from Africa and Asia.
B.    Darwinian theory had little effect on archeology.
C.    All archeological findings were culturally biased in the early 1900s.
D.    Charles Darwin was responsible for the recovery of many artifacts.

9. The tradition of music in the western world originated in the genre of chanting. Chant, a monophonic form of music, was the dominant mode of music prior to the thirteenth century. The semantic origins of the word "monophonic" are of special interest. "Mono" is from a Greek word which means one thing alone or by itself. "Phonic" is also Greek in origin, and it means sound. Accordingly, monophonic music consists of only one sound or voice that combines various notes in a series.

What is the main idea of this passage?
A.    The origins of music in the western world.
B.    The history of music during two previous centuries.
C.    The semantics of a particular Greek word.
D.    The variety of symphonic forms.

10. Various health risks are posed by processed or convenience food. Packaged food often contains chemicals, such as additives to enhance the color of the food or preservatives that give the food a longer life. Food additives are detrimental to health for a number of reasons. First of all, they are not natural and may perhaps be linked to disease in the long term. In addition, they may block the body's ability to absorb energy and nutrients from food, such as essential vitamins and minerals that are required for healthy bodily function.

How does the passage support its claim about food additives?
A.    By explaining their purpose.
B.    By giving reasons for their dangers.
C.    By discussing specific medical case studies.
D.    By linking them to preservatives.

*Read Passages 1 and 2 below. Then answer the questions. You need to answer based on ideas that are stated, suggested, or implied in the passage.*

**Passage 1:**

"Celebrity" is the term used to describe someone who is famous and attracts attention from the general public and the world's media. Traditionally, a celebrity would gain the title by his or her work or achievements in a particular field of expertise. Actors, musicians, politicians, and inventors have all become celebrities in the past. However, as we fall deeper and deeper into the cesspool of the twenty-first century, a new celebrity has arrived – the nobody.

As one peruses glossy TV magazines, it is easy to notice the amount of reality shows that now dominate our screens – Wife Swap, X-Factor, American Idol, America's Got Talent, and the reality pioneer Big Brother. The concept itself of Big Brother is everything that George Orwell warned us about: "normal" people are thrust into the limelight to be mocked, glorified, vilified, and humiliated in equal measures. And we lap it up.

**Passage 2:**

After Big Brother first hit our screens, there were several BB series. However, the housemate that is eventually voted BB winner is not necessarily the most likely to gain fame and fortune from his or her appearance on this cultural phenomenon. The champion of Big Brother earnings, who came in at second place in her series, so far has earned an estimated net worth of three million dollars. While some vilify reality TV shows and the so-called celebrity associated with them, it must nonetheless be noted that participants can change their lives with the potential income levels to be derived from appearing on reality TV.

11. How would the writer of Passage 1 most likely respond to the following statement from Passage 2?: "participants can change their lives with the potential income levels to be derived from appearing on reality TV."
    A. Reality TV participants can earn a great deal of money, but these so-called celebrities have no real achievements or expertise.
    B. Reality TV participants are foolish for wanting to earn money like this.
    C. The general public needs to stop watching reality TV shows in order to avoid money being earned in this way.
    D. Glossy TV magazines should stop promoting reality TV shows.

12. The writer of Passage 2 would criticize the writer of Passage 1 for
    A.    failing to analyze Big Brother in more depth.
    B.    failing to mention any of the positive aspects of reality shows.
    C.    calling the new celebrity a nobody.
    D.    trying to classify people as "normal."

*Read Passages 1 and 2 below. Then answer the questions. You need to answer based on ideas that are stated, suggested, or implied in the passage.*

**Passage 1:**

Resulting from the amazing success of WAP (Wireless Application Protocol) in smart phones and hand-held devices, wireless technology can have an amazing impact on your day-to-day life. These technologies help to make the mobile information society happen by blurring the boundaries between home, the office, and the outside world.

The seamless integration and connectivity that wireless technology brings with it make it possible to work more efficiently. Business users can explore a wide range of interactive services which were difficult to envisage years ago because of the complexity involved in making such devices communicate with each other.

In addition, with wireless technologies, you can get on social media wherever you are, helping us stay connected with friends and family.

**Passage 2:**

Recent research shows that social media platforms may actually be making us antisocial. Survey results indicate that many people would prefer to interact on Facebook or Twitter, rather than see friends and family in person. The primary reason cited for this phenomenon was that one does not need to go to the effort to dress up and travel in order to use these social media platforms.

Another independent survey revealed that people often remain glued to their hand-held devices when they do go out with friends. It therefore seems that social media platforms may be having a detrimental effect on our social skills and interpersonal relationships.

13.  The writer of Passage 1 would most likely criticize the writer of Passage 2 for
    A.   relying on research results rather than anecdotal information.
    B.   placing too much emphasis on certain social media platforms.
    C.   talking about hand-held devices in particular, rather than wireless technology in general.
    D.   overlooking the positive effect that wireless technologies have had on work and office life.

14. The writer of Passage 2 would probably respond to the last sentence in Passage 1 (Now you . . . family.) by
    A. asserting that one should try to balance time spent on social media platforms with time spent in person with loved ones.
    B. pointing out that social media platforms are very convenient.
    C. claiming that we are actually damaging relationships with our friends and family in many cases because of wireless technologies.
    D. arguing that people should leave their hand-held devices at home when going out with friends.

15. The writers of both passages would agree that
    A. wireless technologies have impacted upon society in positive ways.
    B. social media platforms need to be used with caution.
    C. social media platforms have brought about changes to interpersonal relationships.
    D. Facebook and Twitter are useful interactive tools for business users.

*Read the passage and then select the correct answers to the questions. You need to answer based on ideas that are stated, suggested, or implied in the passage.*

**Literary Text 1**

It was the last day of July. The long hot summer was drawing to a close; and we, the weary pilgrims of the London pavement, were beginning to think of the cloud-shadows on the corn-fields, and the autumn breezes on the sea-shore.

For my own poor part, the fading summer left me out of health and out of spirits. During the past year I had not managed my professional resources as carefully as usual; and my extravagance now limited me to the prospect of spending the autumn economically between my mother's cottage at Hampstead and my own chambers in town.

The evening, I remember, was still and cloudy. It was one of the two evenings in every week which I was accustomed to spend with my mother and my sister. So I turned my steps northward in the direction of Hampstead.

The quiet twilight was still trembling on the topmost ridges of the heath; and the view of London below me had sunk into a black gulf in the shadow of the cloudy night, when I stood before the gate of my mother's cottage. I had hardly rung the bell before the house door was opened violently; my worthy Italian friend, Professor Pesca, appeared in the servant's place; and darted out joyously to receive me, with a shrill foreign parody on an English cheer.

I had first become acquainted with my Italian friend by meeting him at certain great houses where he taught his own language and I taught drawing. All I then knew of the history of his life was, that he had once held a situation in the University of Padua; that he had left Italy for political reasons (the nature of which he uniformly declined to mention to any one); and that he had been for many years respectably established in London as a teacher of languages.

I had seen him risk his life in the sea at Brighton. We had met there accidentally, and were bathing together. It never occurred to me that the art which we were practicing might merely add one more to the list of manly exercises which the Professor believed that he could learn impromptu.

16.    What does the narrator suggest in paragraph 2?
   A.    that he has run out of money
   B.    that he has lost all his clients
   C.    that he is suffering from depression
   D.    that he does not get along well with his mother

17. What does the narrator mention his mother and sister in paragraph 3?
    A.     to imply that Hampstead is in a poorer part of the city
    B.     to foreshadow the events that will take place in his mother's cottage
    C.     to indicate a routine
    D.     to create a contrast with Professor Pesca

18. What is the best paraphrase of the following phrase from paragraph 4?:
    "appeared in the servant's place."
    A.     rang the bell for the doorman
    B.     did the job of the doorman
    C.     stood where the servant normally stands
    D.     received the servant's guests

19. What adjective best describes the narrator's relationship with Professor Pesca?
    A.     political
    B.     respectable
    C.     accidental
    D.     collegial

20. What does the narrator state or imply in the last paragraph?
    A.     Professor Pesca saved someone who was drowning.
    B.     Professor Pesca was not prone to impulsive actions.
    C.     Professor Pesca did not know how to swim.
    D.     Professor Pesca had experience working with the Coast Guard.

*Read the passage and then select the correct answers to the questions. You need to answer based on ideas that are stated, suggested, or implied in the passage.*

**Literary Text 2**

Clare, restless, went out into the dusk when evening drew on, she who had won him having retired to her chamber. The night was as sultry as the day. There was no coolness after dark unless on the grass. Roads, garden-paths, the house-fronts, the bartonwalls were warm as earths, and reflected the noontime temperature into the noctambulist's face.

He sat on the east gate of the yard, and knew not what to think of himself. Feeling had indeed smothered judgement that day. Since the sudden embrace, three hours before, the twain had kept apart. She seemed stilled, almost alarmed, at what had occurred, while the novelty, unpremeditation, mastery of circumstance disquieted him— palpitating, contemplative being that he was. He could hardly realize their true relations to each other as yet, and what their mutual bearing should be before third parties thenceforward.

The windows smiled, the door coaxed and beckoned, the creeper blushed confederacy. A personality within it was so far-reaching in her influence as to spread into and make the bricks, mortar, and whole overhanging sky throb with a burning sensibility. Whose was this mighty personality? A milkmaid's.

It was amazing, indeed, to find how great a matter the life of this place had become to him. And though new love was to be held partly responsible for this, it was not solely so. Many have learnt that the magnitude of lives is not as to their external displacements, but as to their subjective experiences. The impressionable peasant leads a larger, fuller, more dramatic life than the king. Looking at it thus, he found that life was to be seen of the same magnitude here as elsewhere.

Despite his heterodoxy, faults, and weaknesses, Clare was a man with a conscience. Tess was no insignificant creature to toy with and dismiss; but a woman living her precious life—a life which, to herself who endured or enjoyed it, possessed as great a dimension as the life of the mightiest to himself. Upon her sensations the whole world depended to Tess; through her existence all her fellow-creatures existed, to her. The universe itself only came into being for Tess on the particular day in the particular year in which she was born.

21. The bartonwalls mentioned in paragraph 1 are most likely
    A.     an area in the garden.
    B.     a feature of the natural landscape.
    C.     a part of the house.
    D.     a path leading to one of the roads.

22. What is the meaning of the word "noctambulist" as it is used in the passage?
   A.   a person who suddenly falls in love
   B.   a person who responds impulsively to subjective experiences
   C.   a person who experiences an external displacement
   D.   a person who goes for a walk after dark

23. What is the best paraphrase of the following statement from paragraph 2: "what their mutual bearing should be before third parties thenceforward"?
   A.   how they should behave to each other around other people
   B.   whether or not they should support each other as a couple from this moment onwards
   C.   whether or not they should kiss each other in public
   D.   how they should decide whom to tell that they are now a couple

24. Where does the story take place?
   A.   in a royal court
   B.   in a peasant's abode
   C.   in a dairy farm
   D.   in a manor house

25. What does the narrator imply when he states that "Clare was a man with a conscience"?
   A.   Clare has behaved poorly towards women in the past, but he repents of this behavior.
   B.   Clare knows that Tess is hypersensitive, but she has to be aware of his needs.
   C.   Clare understands that his life in his current environment may not be of the same magnitude that he has experienced in the past.
   D.   Clare realizes that he needs to treat Tess well because she has had her own life experiences, both positive and negative.

# TSI READING PRACTICE TEST 3 – ANSWERS AND EXPLANATIONS

1. The correct answer is C. We know that the passage is going to give historical information because the topic sentence [defined as the first sentence of a paragraph] contains the phrase "was founded in 1876." Answers A and B give specific points that are mentioned in the passage, not the main idea. Answer D is incorrect because no criticisms are stated in the passage.

2. The correct answer is A. The passage states that "computer-to-computer trading could result in a downturn in the stock market." Further, this downturn could result in a "computer-led stock market crash." In order to avoid these negative results, the regulations are needed. Answers B and C are not stated in the passage. Answer D is incorrect because the passage talks about how the use of computers has *changed* over time.

3. The correct answer is C. The last sentence of the passage explains the purpose of or reasons for the aircraft crash investigations. Answers A and B are too specific. Answer D is not stated in the passage.

4. The correct answer is C. The last sentence of the passage states: "It took an expedition of Italian scientists, who used a surfeit of technological devices, to disprove Wallerstein's claim." In other words, the Italians proved that Everest was in fact higher than K-2. [Note: *Surfeit* means a large or abundant amount of something.]

5. The correct answer is A. The words "sinister undertones" and "arguably" in the passage demonstrate that cloning is a controversial subject. Answer C is not implied in the passage. There is no information in the passage to suggest that answers B and D are correct.

6. The correct answer is D. The passage uses the words "myths," "misconceptions," and "mistakenly" to show that most people do not have the correct knowledge about tornadoes.

7. The correct answer is B. When explaining the idea of assimilation, the passage uses the phrase "are examples of" to show that breast and bottle feeding are being used as examples. Note that "exemplify" means to give an example.

8. The correct answer is A. The passage concludes by stating: "there was a surge in artifacts excavated from African and Asian localities by the late 1900s." "Surge" means to increase suddenly from a small or low amount. If these findings suddenly increased at the end of the century, one could assume that they were limited at the beginning of the century. Answers B and D are incorrect according to the passage. Answer C is an overgeneralization.

9. The correct answer is A. The topic sentence contains the word "originated." Only one century is mentioned in the passage, so answer B is incorrect. Answer C is too specific. Answer D is not stated in the passage.

10. The correct answer is B. The passage states: "Food additives are detrimental to health for a number of reasons." This statement is followed by two reasons: the link to disease and the blockage of nutrients.

11. The correct answer is A. The writer of passage 1 states that "Traditionally, a celebrity would gain the title by his or her work or achievements in a particular field of expertise," so he would agree with answer A.

12. The correct answer is B. The writer of passage 2 describes how participants in reality shows can "change their lives with the potential income levels to be derived from appearing on reality TV." This is an assertion about the positive, life-changing aspects of reality television. The writer of passage 1 fails to discuss any positive aspects of reality TV.

13. The correct answer is D. The writer of passage 1 talks about office life in paragraph 1 and about business users in paragraph 2. The writer of passage 2 does not mention these aspects of wireless technology.

14. The correct answer is C. The writer of passage 2 explains how people are more inclined to stay at home to chat on social media than to go out with friends and how people are glued to their hand-held devices even when they are out with friends. These are two detrimental impacts of social media on interpersonal relationships.

15. The correct answer is C. The writer of passage 1 describes the positive changes, while the writer of passage 2 describes the negative changes.

16. The correct answer is A. The narrator states in paragraph 2 that he needs to spend the autumn "economically," so the reader can surmise that he is having financial problems. Note that the narrator mentions that he is "out of spirits," but this condition is not as serious as suffering from depression.

17. The correct answer is C. The narrator says: "It was one of the two evenings in every week which I was accustomed to spend with my mother and my sister." The word "accustomed" indicates that a routine is being described.

18. The correct answer is B. The doorman would have been the servant who welcomed visitors at the front door of the house.

19. The correct answer is D. "Collegial" means acting like colleagues, or people who work in the same profession. Paragraph 5 of the text explains that Professor Pesca and the narrator met when they were teachers, so the two characters would have been colleagues.

20. The correct answer is C. The last paragraph tells us that swimming was one of the "manly exercises which the Professor believed that he could learn impromptu." The word "impromptu" means "on the spot" or "without previous practice or experience."

21. The correct answer is C. The description moves from the roads, to the garden, and then to the house. In other words, the description moves from the outdoors to the house itself, so the bartonwalls are probably a part of the house.

22. The correct answer is D. Paragraph 1 mentions that it is after dusk and that it was nighttime. We also know from paragraph 1 that Clare was restless and that he had gone out.

23. The correct answer is A. "Mutual bearing" means how they interact with each other. "Third parties" is a formal way of saying "other people."

24. The correct answer is C. The know that the story takes place in a dairy farm because Clare confesses that he has fallen in love with a milkmaid at the end of paragraph 3.

25. The correct answer is D. In the next sentence of the paragraph, the narrator tells us that "Tess was no insignificant creature to toy with and dismiss; but a woman living her precious life—a life which, to herself who endured or enjoyed it, possessed as great a dimension as the life of the mightiest to himself." This sentence describes both the positive and negative experiences in Tess's life. It implies that Clare needs to respect Tess when it states that she "was no insignificant creature to toy with and dismiss."

**TSI WRITING PRACTICE TEST 3**

*Read the draft essay below and then choose the best answers to the questions that follow.*

(*1*) Organic farming and organic produce create many positive outcomes for the environment.

(*2*) Most mainstream American consumers have reservations about organic food.

(*3*) The first drawback that consumers perceive is of course the cost. (*4*) Consumers with higher income levels can afford organically-grown food, but many people simply do not believe that these are worth the added expense.

(*5*) There also concerns about the safety of organic food due to using cow manure and the use of other animal waste as fertilizer. (*6*) Take the case of windfall apples, which are apples that fall off the tree, these apples can be contaminated by the cow manure. (*7*) This contamination occurs because manure contains a virulent bacterium. (*8*) This bacterium is known as e-coli.

(*9*) Some people are reluctant to purchase organic food because they believe that it spoils too quickly. (*10*) Therefore, it may be quite some time before the purchase of organic food became the norm in American households.

    1.      What is the best way to revise and combine sentences 1 and 2?

        A.      Organic farming and organic produce create many positive outcomes for the environment, most mainstream American consumers have reservations about organic food.

        B.      Most mainstream American consumers have reservations about organic food; yet organic farming and organic produce create many positive outcomes for the environment.

C.    While organic farming and organic produce create many positive outcomes for the environment, most mainstream American consumers have reservations about organic food.

D.    Organic farming and organic produce create many positive outcomes for the environment, even though most mainstream American consumers have reservations about organic food.

2.    What is the best way to punctuate sentence 3?

A.    The first drawback that consumers perceive is of course the cost.
B.    The first drawback that consumers perceive is, of course the cost.
C.    The first drawback that consumers perceive is of course, the cost.
D.    The first drawback that consumers perceive is, of course, the cost.

3.    Which of the following sentences would be best inserted between sentences 3 and 4?
A.    However, there are also certain advantages to organic food.
B.    Organic food often costs 50 to 100 percent more than food produced using traditional farming methods.
C.    Organic farming procedures in European countries are quite different than American procedures.
D.    Business acumen is required of the organic farmer in order to understand effective market strategies.

4.    What is the error in sentence 4? Sentence 4 is provided again here for ease of reference.

*Consumers with higher income levels can afford organically-grown food, but many people simply do not believe that these are worth the added expense.*

A.    The words "can afford" should be replaced with the words "should afford"
B.    The words "with higher income levels" should be replaced with the words "at higher level income"
C.    The word "these" should be replaced with the word "they"
D.    The words "these are" should be replaced with the words "it is"

5.    Where is the best place to insert the following sentence?

*Consumption of the contaminated fruit can lead to serious food poisoning or even death if the produce is not washed correctly.*

A.    After sentence 5
B.    After sentence 6
C.    After sentence 7
D.    After sentence 8

6. What is the best revision to the phrase "due to using cow manure and the use of other animal waste" in sentence 5?

   A. due to the using of cow manure and other animal waste
   B. due to the use of cow manure and using other animal waste
   C. due to the use of cow manure and other animal waste
   D. due to using cow manure and using other animal waste

7. What is one possible way to rewrite sentence 6? Sentence 6 is provided again here for ease of reference.

   *Take the case of windfall apples, which are apples that fall off the tree, these apples can be contaminated by the cow manure.*

   A. Place a period after the word "tree" and capitalize the word "these" to begin a new sentence.
   B Remove the comma after "apples" and replace the word "which" with the word "that"
   C. Replace the phrase "which are apples that fall" with the word "falling"
   D. Delete the word "the" before the phrase "cow manure"

8. What is the best way to revise and combine sentences 7 and 8?

   A. This contamination occurs because manure contains a virulent bacterium known as e-coli.
   B. Known as e-coli, this contamination occurs because manure contains a virulent bacterium.
   C. This contamination, known as e-coli, occurs because manure contains a virulent bacterium.
   D. This contamination occurs, known as e-coli, because manure contains a virulent bacterium.

9. Which one of the following words or phrases would be best inserted at the beginning of sentence 9? Sentence 9 is provided again here for ease of reference.

   *Some people are reluctant to purchase organic food because they believe that it spoils too quickly.*

   A. Namely,
   B. For instance,
   C. Last but not least,
   D. In general,

10.  What is the best way to revise sentence 10? Sentence 10 is provided again here for ease of reference.

*Therefore, it may be quite some time before the purchase of organic food became the norm in American households.*

A.  Delete the word "quite"
B.  Replace the word "purchase" with the word "purchasing"
C.  Insert the word "the" before the word "American"
D.  Replace the word "became" with the word "becomes"

*Select the best substitute for the underlined parts of the following ten sentences. The first answer [choice A] is identical to the original sentence. If you think the original sentence is best, then choose A as your answer.*

11.  While at the mall, <u>a paperback book was purchased by me.</u>
A.  a paperback book was purchased by me.
B.  the paperback book was purchased by me.
C.  a paperback book's purchase was made by me.
D.  I purchased a paperback book.

12.  <u>We just arrived</u> at the airport when Tom's flight landed.
A.  We just arrived
B.  Just had we arrived
C.  We had just arrived
D.  Just we were arriving

13.  We were going to go away on <u>vacation. And then</u> our plans changed.
A.  Vacation. And then
B.  vacation, then
C.  vacation and then
D.  vacation, and then

14.  John's favorite hobbies are <u>to read and to swim.</u>
A.  to read and to swim.
B.  to read and swimming.
C.  reading and swimming.
D.  reading and to swim.

15.  <u>Exasperated, Bill finally lost his temper</u> with his unruly children.
A.  Exasperated, Bill finally lost his temper
B.  Bill was exasperated, finally lost his temper
C.  Bill, was exasperated, finally lost his temper
D.  Exasperating Bill, finally lost

16. He was planning on finding a new <u>apartment that</u> would accommodate all of his oversized furniture.
    A.    apartment that
    B.    apartment. One that
    C.    apartment, that
    D.    apartment so that

17. "I can't believe you won the <u>lottery", Sarah</u> exclaimed.
    A.    lottery", Sarah
    B.    lottery." Sarah
    C.    lottery!" Sarah
    D.    lottery" Sarah

18. <u>In spite of he studied hard, he</u> failed the exam.
    A.    In spite of he studied hard, he
    B.    In spite of studying hard, he
    C.    In spite of he studying hard, he
    D.    In spite of studied hard, he

19. Jane is the <u>taller of</u> her four sisters.
    A.    taller of
    B.    taller than
    C.    most tall of
    D.    tallest of

20. <u>If stealing money from your employer,</u> you could be charged with the crime of embezzlement.
    A.    If stealing money from your employer,
    B.    Stealing money from your employer
    C.    If you steal money from your employer,
    D.    If you steal money from your employer

*Rewrite the following ten sentences mentally in your own head. Follow the directions given for the formation of the new sentence. Remember that your new sentence should be grammatically correct and convey the same meaning as the original sentence.*

21. After checking the extent of the man's injuries, the paramedics put him into the ambulance. Rewrite, beginning with: <u>Once they</u>

    The next words will be:
    A.    were checking
    B.    had checked
    C.    had been checking
    D.    will check

22. The professor's praise of my exam score in front of the other students embarrassed me. Rewrite, beginning with: <u>I was embarrassed when</u>

   The next words will be:
   A.     the professor praised
   B.     the professor praising
   C.     the professor, praising
   D.     the professor, he praised

23. Both Minnesota and Wisconsin get extremely cold in the winter. Rewrite, beginning with: <u>Like Minnesota,</u>

   The next words will be:
   A.     Wisconsin gets
   B.     and Wisconsin
   C.     extreme cold
   D.     it is

24. Rich in natural beauty and abundant in wildlife, the Grand Canyon is a popular tourist destination. Rewrite, beginning with: <u>The Grand Canyon</u>

   Your new sentence will include:
   A.     because being
   B.     because it being
   C.     because it is
   D.     because being it

25. My sister was ill with the flu, so she stayed home from school. Rewrite, beginning with: <u>My sister,</u>

   The next words will be:
   A.     ill and
   B.     she was ill
   C.     was ill
   D.     who was ill

26. If it rains tomorrow, we will have to cancel the picnic. Rewrite, beginning with: <u>In the event of</u>

   The next words will be:
   A.     raining
   B.     rains
   C.     rain
   D.     it rains

27. The team lost the championship game, and the players were so disappointed. Rewrite, beginning with: <u>The team was</u>

   Your new sentence will include:
   A.    although it lost
   B.    when it lost
   C.    and it lost
   D.    because the loss of

28. Despite years of training, he was not selected for the Olympics. Rewrite, beginning with: <u>Although</u>

   The next words will be:
   A.    he trained for years
   B.    training for years
   C.    years of training
   D.    years he trained

29. As he watched television, he fell asleep and began snoring. Rewrite, beginning with: <u>Watching</u>

   The next words will be:
   A.    television he fell
   B.    and fell
   C.    television, he fell
   D.    television, and falling

30. Many international students suffer from homesickness during their studies in the United States. Rewrite, beginning with: <u>Suffering from</u>

   Your new sentence will include:
   A.    common international student's
   B.    is common studying
   C.    is commonality of international students
   D.    is common among international students

# TSI WRITING PRACTICE TEST 3 – ANSWERS AND EXPLANATIONS

1. The correct answer is C. This is another example of how to subordinate two sentences.

2. The correct answer is D. The phrase "of course" needs to be preceded and followed by commas when used in the middle of a sentence like this.

3. The correct answer is B. We are talking here about the cost of organic food, so the new sentence needs to address this topic.

4. The correct answer is D. "Food" is a singular noun, so the singular pronoun "it" is needed here.

5. The correct answer is B. We are speaking about the apples at this juncture, so the new sentence must be placed after sentence 6, which also talks about the apples.

6. The correct answer is C. This is another question on parallelism, which means that you have to use the same form when giving items in a list or series. Answers A and B are not the best because we can put "use" or "using" in the new sentence, but not both forms. Sentence D is not the best answer because it is repetitious.

7. The correct answer is A. "These apples can be contaminated by the cow manure" is a complete sentence, so the word "these" needs to be capitalized. The sentence preceding it needs to end in a period to avoid making a comma splice.

8. The correct answer is A. E-coli describes the bacterium, not the contamination, so the phrase "known as e-coli" needs to be placed after the word "bacterium". The other sentences misplace the modifier.

9. The correct answer is C. The text has talked about the disadvantages of organic food. We are talking here about the final disadvantage, so we need a phrase to indicate that we are drawing the discussion to a close.

10. The correct answer is D. We are making a prediction about a habitual action in the future, so we need to use the present simple tense of the verb "becomes".

11. The correct answer is D. The phrase *while at the mall* modifies the pronoun "I." So, "I" needs to come after this phrase.

12. The correct answer is C. When a compound sentence contains the word "just" to describe an action that has recently been completed, the past perfect tense [had + past participle] should be used in the part of the sentence containing the word "just."

13. The correct answer is D. This question is about the use of punctuation. "Then our plans changed" is an independent clause. It has a grammatical subject [our plans] and a verb [changed]. According to traditional rules of grammar, "and" is a coordinating conjunction, used to combine phrases or clauses within a sentence. Since "and" is a conjunction, we should avoid beginning sentences with "and." So, the word "and" should be included within a single sentence and preceded by a comma.

14. The correct answer is C. This question is about gerunds, also known as -ing words or verbal nouns. Note that the -ing form is usually used when discussing activities or hobbies.

15. The correct answer is A. Exasperated is a past participle phrase that describes Bill. So, the sentence is correct as it is written.

16. The correct answer is A. The words "that would accommodate all of his oversized furniture" form a dependent relative clause. A dependent relative clause containing "that" is not preceded by a comma.

17. The correct answer is C. Punctuation should be enclosed within the final quotation mark when giving dialogue. The word *exclaimed* shows that the exclamation point is needed.

18. The correct answer is B. The phrase "in spite of" must be followed by a noun or noun phrase. "In spite of" should not be followed by a clause. The -ing form "studying" is used as a gerund (a verbal noun) in this sentence.

19. The correct answer is D. This question tests your knowledge of the comparative and superlative forms. Use the comparative form (-er) when comparing two things. If you are comparing more than two things, you must use the superlative form (-est).

20. The correct answer is C. This question tests your knowledge of conditional sentence structures. Conditional sentences often begin with the word *if*. Conditional sentences may address hypothetical or imaginary situations. This sentence mentions a hypothetical situation. Therefore, the simple present tense (steal) is used in the "If" clause, and the modal verb (could) is used in the main part of the sentence. The two parts of conditional sentences beginning with "if" must be separated by a comma.

21. The correct answer is B. The new sentence is: Once they had checked the extent of the man's injuries, the paramedics put him into the ambulance. Clauses that begin with "once" need to contain the past perfect tense. The past perfect tense is formed with "had" plus the past participle, which is "checked" in this sentence.

22. The correct answer is A. The new sentence is: I was embarrassed when the professor praised my exam score in front of the other students. The word "when" forms a subordinate clause in the second part of the new sentence. Since the first part of the new sentence contains the past tense (was), the second part of the new sentence also contains the past tense (praised). The words "the professor" form the grammatical subject of the subordinate clause. Therefore, the pronoun "he" is not needed.

23. The correct answer is A. The new sentence is: Like Minnesota, Wisconsin gets extremely cold in the winter. The phrase "like Minnesota" is an adjectival phrase that modifies the noun "Wisconsin." Therefore, "Wisconsin" must come directly after the comma.

24. The correct answer is C. The new sentence is: The Grand Canyon is a popular tourist destination because it is rich in natural beauty and abundant in wildlife. The word "because" is used to join a subordinate clause to a sentence. Remember that clauses are distinct from phrases because clauses contain both a grammatical subject and a verb. "It" is the grammatical subject in the subordinate clause of the new sentence and "is" is the verb.

25. The correct answer is D. The new sentence is: My sister, who was ill with the flu, stayed home from school. The comma after "my sister" indicates that a relative clause must be used. Remember that relative clauses can include the following words: who, which, that, whom, whose.

26. The correct answer is C. The new sentence is: In the event of rain tomorrow, the picnic will have to be canceled. The phrase "in the event of" should be followed by a noun or noun phrase. In addition, the verb must be changed to the passive from, using the verb "be."

27. The correct answer is B. The new sentence would be constructed as follows: The team was so disappointed when it lost the championship game.

28. The correct answer is A. The new sentence would be constructed as follows: Although he trained for years, he was not selected for the Olympics. Sentences that begin with "although" introduce an unexpected result to a situation.

29. The correct answer is C. The new sentence is: Watching television, he fell asleep and began snoring. Phrases that begin with verbs in the -ing form are known as present participle phrases. In the new sentence, the present participle phrase "watching television" modifies "he." Therefore, "he" must come directly after the comma.

30. The correct answer is D. The new sentence is as follows: Suffering from homesickness is common among international students who study in the United States. In the new sentence, the -ing form (suffering) is used as a gerund. So, "suffering from homesickness" is the grammatical subject of the new sentence. The grammatical subject is followed by a verb (is) and an adjective (common). Note that "commonality" is a noun.

# TSI TEXAS SUCCESS INITIATIVE – ESSAY WRITING GUIDE

## Essay Structure

Most teachers agree that the best essays follow a four or five paragraph format. This format will help to insure that your essay is well-organized. This format also helps you write longer and more developed essays.

The five paragraph essay is organized as follows:

Paragraph 1 – This paragraph is the introduction to your essay. It should include a thesis statement that clearly indicates your main idea. It should also give the reader an overview of your supporting points. A thesis statement is a sentence that asserts the main idea of your essay.

The best thesis statements are those that contain a central idea that will serve to narrow the focus of the essay and control the flow ideas within it. As such, a thesis statement should not be too general or vague.

A good structure for the thesis statement is to think of it in terms of an assertion plus a reason or explanation. This structure is better than just giving your assertion or opinion on its own because your explanation indicates the direction that your writing is going to take.

You can think of the essay introduction like a funnel: wide at the top and narrow at the bottom. In other words, start off your introduction in a general but interesting way, and then narrow it down to your main idea and specific supporting points. Remember that the introduction announces your main idea and supporting points, while your main body develops them.

Paragraph 2 – The second paragraph is where you elaborate on your first supporting point. It is normally recommended that you state your strongest and most persuasive point in this paragraph.

Paragraph 3 – You should elaborate on your main idea in the third paragraph by providing a second supporting point.

Paragraph 4 – You should mention your third supporting point in the fourth paragraph. This can be the supporting point that you feel to be the weakest.

Paragraph 5 – In the fifth and final paragraph of the essay, you should make your conclusion. The conclusion should reiterate your supporting points and sum up your position.

The four paragraph essay will follow the same structure as above, with paragraphs 2 and 3 elaborating two key supporting points and paragraph 4 stating the conclusion. If you decide to put four paragraphs in your essay instead of five, each paragraph should be longer and slightly more detailed than that of a five paragraph essay.

**Essay FAQs**

How long should each body paragraph be?

For a four paragraph essay, each body paragraph should range from 120 to 170 words. For a five paragraph essay, each body paragraph should be from 100 to 140 words.

What is an elaborating idea?

Elaborating ideas include both explanations and examples. Providing clear examples to support your points is extremely important.

Each of your main body paragraphs should contain an example that supports your line of argument.

You should elaborate on and explain your example in order to make your essay persuasive.

How do elaborating ideas help to raise my essay score?

Elaboration lengthens your essay and gives you more opportunities to demonstrate higher-level grammar, complex sentence construction, and academic vocabulary.

How many elaborating ideas should I have in each paragraph?

This roughly equates to two or three elaborating ideas for each body paragraph.

How do I write the conclusion to the essay?

Conclusions can consist of as few as two sentences, provided that the sentences are cohesive, coherent, and well-constructed.

As in other parts of your essay, you will need to reiterate certain concepts in the conclusion, without repeating word for word what you have already written.

## Using Linking Words and Subordination to Build Sentences

In order to perform well on the essay component of the exam, you will need to write long and developed sentences.

Sentence linking words can help you combine short sentences together to create more complex sentence structures.

Sentence linking words and phrases fall into three categories: sentence linkers, phrase linkers, and subordinators.

In order to understand how to use these types of sentence linking words and phrases correctly, you will need to know some basics of English grammar.

The basic grammatical principles for these concepts are explained in this section. Be sure to study the examples carefully before you attempt the exercises in the following section.

TYPE 1 – SENTENCE LINKERS:

Sentence linkers are used to link two complete sentences together. A complete sentence is one that has a grammatical subject and a verb.

Sentence linkers are usually placed at the beginning of a sentence and are followed by a comma.

They can also be preceded by a semicolon and followed by a comma when joining two sentences together. When doing so, the first letter of the first word of the second sentence must not be capitalized.

Sentence linker examples:

You need to enjoy your time at college. *However*, you should still study hard.

You need to enjoy your time at college; *however*, you should still study hard.

In the examples above, the grammatical subject of the first sentence is "you" and the verb is "need to enjoy".

In the second sentence, "you" is the grammatical subject and "should study" is the verb.

TYPE 2 – PHRASE LINKERS:

In order to understand the difference between phrase linkers and sentence linkers, you must first be able to distinguish a sentence from a phrase.

A phrase linker must be followed by a phrase, while a sentence linker must be followed by a sentence.

The basic distinction between phrases and sentences is that phrases do not have both grammatical subjects and verbs, while sentences contain grammatical subjects and verbs.

*Here are some examples of phrases:*

Her beauty and grace

Life's little problems

A lovely summer day in the month of June

Working hard

Being desperate for money

Note that the last two phrases above use the –ing form, known in these instances as the present participle.

Present participle phrases, which are often used to modify nouns or pronouns, are sometimes placed at the beginning of sentences as introductory phrases.

*Here are some examples of sentences:*

Mary worked all day long.

My sister lives in Seattle.

Wintertime is brutal in Montana.

"Mary," "my sister," and "wintertime" are the grammatical subjects of the above sentences.

Remember that verbs are words that show action or states of being, so "worked," "lives," and "is" are the verbs in the three sentences above.

Look at the examples that follow:

Phrase linker example 1 – no comma: He received a promotion *because of* his dedication to the job.

"His dedication to the job" is a noun phrase.

<u>Phrase linker example 2 – with comma:</u> *Because of* his dedication to the job, he received a promotion.

When the sentence begins with the phrase linker, we classify the sentence as an inverted sentence.

Notice that you will need to place a comma between the two parts of the sentence when it is inverted.

TYPE 3 – SUBORDINATORS:

Subordinators must be followed by an independent clause. Subordinators cannot be followed by a phrase.

The two clauses of a subordinated sentence must be separated by a comma.

The structure of independent clauses is similar to that of sentences because independent clauses contain a grammatical subject and a verb.

<u>Subordinator examples:</u>

*Although* he worked hard, he failed to make his business profitable.

He failed to make his business profitable, *although* he worked hard.

There are two clauses: "He worked hard" and "he failed to make his business profitable."

The grammatical subjects in each clause are the words "he", while the verbs are "worked" and "failed."

*Now look at the sentence linking words and phrases below. Note which ones are sentence linkers, which ones are phrase linkers, and which ones are subordinators.*

*Then refer to the rules above to remember the grammatical principles for sentence linkers, phrase linkers, and subordinators.*

<u>Sentence linkers for giving additional information</u>

further

furthermore

apart from this

what is more

in addition

additionally

in the same way

moreover

## Sentence linkers for giving examples

for example

for instance

in this case

in particular

more precisely

namely

in brief

in short

## Sentence linkers for stating the obvious

obviously

clearly

naturally

of course

surely

after all

## Sentence linkers for giving generalizations

in general

on the whole

as a rule

for the most part

generally speaking

in most cases

<u>Sentence linkers for stating causes and effects</u>

thus

accordingly

hence

therefore

in that case

under those circumstances

as a result

for this reason

as a consequence

consequently

in effect

<u>Sentence linkers for concession or unexpected results</u>

however

nevertheless

meanwhile

<u>Sentence linkers for giving conclusions</u>

finally

to conclude

lastly

in conclusion

Sentence linkers for contrast

on the other hand

on the contrary

alternatively

rather

Sentence linkers for paraphrasing or restating

in other words

that is to say

that is

Sentence linkers for showing similarity

similarly

in the same way

likewise

Phrase linkers for giving additional information

besides

in addition to

Phrase linkers for stating causes and effects

because of

due to

owing to

## Phrase linkers for concession or unexpected results

despite

in spite of

## Phrase linkers for comparison

compared to

like

## Phrase linkers for contrast

in contrast to

instead of

rather than

without

## Subordinators

although

as

because

but

due to the fact that

even though

since

so

so that

once

unless

until

when

whereas

while

not only . . . but also

Time words that can be used both as phrase linkers and subordinators

after

before

Special cases

yet –"Yet" can be used as both a subordinator and as a sentence linker.

in order to – "In order to" must be followed by the base form of the verb.

thereby – "Thereby" must be followed by the present participle.

## Using Linking Words and Subordination to Build Sentences – Exercises

*Look at the pairs of sentences in the exercises below. Make new sentences, using the phrase linkers, sentence linkers, and subordinators provided. In many cases, you will need to create one single sentence from the two sentences provided. You may need to change or delete some of the words in the original sentences.*

**Exercise 1:**

The temperature was quite high yesterday.

It really didn't feel that hot outside.

*Write new sentences beginning as follows:*

a) In spite of . . .

Hint: You need to change the form of the verb "was" in answer (a).

b) The temperature . . .

You need to include the word "nevertheless" in answer (b). Be careful with punctuation and capitalization in your answer.

**Exercise 2:**

Our star athlete didn't receive a gold medal in the Olympics.

He had trained for competition for several years in advance.

*Write new sentences beginning as follows:*

a) Our star athlete . . . .

Answer (a) should contain the word "although."

b) Despite . . .

**Exercise 3:**

There are acrimonious relationships within our extended family.

Our immediate family decided to go away on vacation during the holiday season to avoid these conflicts.

*Write new sentences beginning as follows:*

a) Because of . . .

b) Because . . .

c) Due to the fact that  . . .

**Exercise 4:**

My best friend had been feeling extremely sick for several days.

She refused to see the doctor.

*Write new sentences beginning as follows:*

a) My best friend . . .

Answer (a) should contain the word "however."

b) My best friend . . .

Answer (b) should contain the word "but."

Be careful with capitalization and punctuation in your answers.

**Exercise 5:**

He generally doesn't like drinking alcohol.

He will do so on social occasions.

*Write new sentences beginning as follows:*

a) While . . .

b) He generally . . .

Answer (b) should contain the word "yet."

**Exercise 6:**

The government's policies failed to stimulate spending and expand economic growth.

The country slipped further into recession.

*Write new sentences beginning as follows:*

a) The government's policies . . .

Answer (a) should contain the word "thus."

b) The government's policies . . .

Answer (b) should contain the word "so."

## Exercise 7:

Students may attend certain classes without fulfilling a prerequisite.

Students are advised of the benefit of taking at least one non-required introductory course.

*Write new sentences beginning as follows:*

a) Even though  . . .

b) Students may attend . . .

Answer (b) should contain the phrase "apart from this."

## Exercise 8:

There have been advances in technology and medical science.

Infant mortality rates have declined substantially in recent years.

*Write new sentences beginning as follows:*

a) Owing to . . .

b) Since . . .

## Exercise 9:

It was the most expensive restaurant in town.

It had rude staff and provided the worst service.

*Write new sentences beginning as follows:*

a) It was the most . . .

Answer (a) should contain the word "besides."

b) In addition to . . .

**Exercise 10:**

*Now try to combine these three sentences:*

The judge did not punish the criminal justly.

He decided to grant a lenient sentence.

He did not send out a message to deter potential offenders in the future.

*Write new sentences as follows:*

a) Instead of . . . and thereby . . .

b) Rather than . . .  in order to . . .

Before you attempt your answer, look for the cause and effect relationships among the three sentences.

In other words, which event came first? Which ones were second and third in the chain of events?

Also be careful with punctuation in your answers.

**Using Linking Words and Subordination to Build Sentences – Answers**

**Exercise 1:**

The temperature was quite high yesterday.

It really didn't feel that hot outside.

**Answer (a):**

a) In spite of the temperature being quite high yesterday, it really didn't feel that hot outside.

The words "in spite of" are a phrase linker, not a sentence linker.

That is to say, "in spite of" needs to be followed by a phrase, not a clause.

The verb "was" needs to be changed to "being" in order to form a present participle phrase.

Present participle phrases are made by using the –ing form of the verb. We will see this construction again in some of the following answers.

**Answer (b):**

There are two possible answers:

b) The temperature was quite high yesterday. Nevertheless, it really didn't feel that hot outside.

b) The temperature was quite high yesterday; nevertheless, it really didn't feel that hot outside.

"Nevertheless" is a sentence linker. As such, it needs to be used to begin a new sentence.

Alternatively, the semicolon can be used to join the original sentences. If the semicolon is used, the first letter of the word following it must not be capitalized.

**Exercise 2:**

Our star athlete didn't receive a gold medal in the Olympics.

He had trained for competition for several years in advance.

**Answer (a):**

a) Our star athlete didn't receive a gold medal in the Olympics, although he had trained for competition for several years in advance

"Although" is a subordinator, so the two sentences can be combined without any changes.

**Answer (b):**

b) Despite having trained for competition for several years in advance, our star athlete didn't receive a gold medal in the Olympics.

"Despite" is a phrase linker. As we have seen in answer (a) of exercise 1 above, phrase linkers need to be followed by phrases, not clauses.

The two parts of the sentence are inverted, and the verb "had" needs to be changed to "having" to make the present participle form.

**Exercise 3:**

There are acrimonious relationships within our extended family.

Our immediate family decided to go away on vacation during the holiday season to avoid these conflicts.

**Answer (a):**

a) Because of acrimonious relationships within our extended family, our immediate family decided to go away on vacation during the holiday season to avoid these conflicts.

"Because of" is a phrase linker. As such, the subject and verb (there are) need to be removed from the original sentence in order to form a phrase.

**Answer (b):**

b) Because there are acrimonious relationships within our extended family, our immediate family decided to go away on vacation during the holiday season to avoid these conflicts.

**Answer (c):**

c) Due to the fact that there are acrimonious relationships within our extended family, our immediate family decided to go away on vacation during the holiday season to avoid these conflicts.

"Because" and "due to the fact that" are subordinators, so no changes to the original sentences are required.

The phrase "to avoid these conflicts" can be omitted since this idea is already implied by the words "acrimonious relationships."

**Exercise 4:**

My best friend had been feeling extremely sick for several days.

She refused to see the doctor.

**Answer (a):**

There are two possible answers.

a) My best friend had been feeling extremely sick for several days. However, she refused to see the doctor.

a) My best friend had been feeling extremely sick for several days; however, she refused to see the doctor.

Like "nevertheless" in exercise 1, the word "however" is a sentence linker. Remember that sentence linkers need to be used at the beginning of a new sentence.

Alternatively, the semicolon can be used to join the original sentences. If the semicolon is used, "however" must not begin with a capital letter and needs to be followed by a comma.

**Answer (b):**

b) My best friend had been feeling extremely sick for several days, but she refused to see the doctor.

"But" is a subordinator, so the two sentences can be combined without any changes.

**Exercise 5:**

He generally doesn't like drinking alcohol.

He will do so on social occasions.

**Answer (a):**

a) While he generally doesn't like drinking alcohol, he will do so on social occasions.

Like "although," the word "while" is a subordinator, so no changes to the original sentences are needed.

**Answer (b):**

"Yet" can be used as both a subordinator and as a sentence linker, so there are three possible answers in this instance.

When used as a sentence linker, the sentence construction is similar to the sentences containing nevertheless" from exercise 1 and "however" from exercise 4.

Accordingly, these are two possible answers:

b) He doesn't like drinking alcohol. Yet, he will do so on social occasions.

b) He doesn't like drinking alcohol; yet, he will do so on social occasions.

A third possible answer is to use "yet" as a subordinator:

b) He doesn't like drinking alcohol, yet he will do so on social occasions.

The difference is that the third sentence places slightly less emphasis on the particular occasions in which he will drink than the other two sentences.

**Exercise 6:**

The government's policies failed to stimulate spending and expand economic growth.

The country slipped further into recession.

**Answer (a):**

"Thus" is a sentence linker, so there are two possible answers:

a) The government's policies failed to stimulate spending and expand economic growth. Thus, the country slipped further into recession.

a) The government's policies failed to stimulate spending and expand economic growth; thus, the country slipped further into recession.

**Answer (b):**

b) The government's policies failed to stimulate spending and expand economic growth, so the country slipped further into recession.

"So" is a subordinator. The two sentences may therefore be joined without any changes.

**Exercise 7:**

Students may attend certain classes without fulfilling a prerequisite.

Students are advised of the benefit of taking at least one non-required introductory course.

**Answer (a):**

There are two possible answers.

a) Even though students may attend certain classes without fulfilling a prerequisite, they are advised of the benefit of taking at least one non-required introductory course.

a) Even though students are advised of the benefit of taking at least one non-required introductory course, they may attend certain classes without fulfilling a prerequisite.

"Even though" is a subordinator, so no changes are needed. It is advisable to change the word "students" to the pronoun "they" on the second part of the new sentence in order to avoid repetition.

The order or the clauses may be changed in the new sentence since there is no cause and effect relationship between the two original sentences.

**Answer (b):**

There are two possible answers:

b) Students may attend certain classes without fulfilling a prerequisite. Apart from this, they are advised of the benefit of taking at least one non-required introductory course.

b) Students may attend certain classes without fulfilling a prerequisite; apart from this, they are advised of the benefit of taking at least one non-required introductory course.

"Apart from this" is a sentence linker, so it needs to be used at the beginning of a separate sentence.

**Exercise 8:**

There have been advances in technology and medical science.

Infant mortality rates have declined substantially in recent years.

**Answer (a):**

a) Owing to advances in technology and medical science, infant mortality rates have declined substantially in recent years.

"Owing to" is a phrase linker that shows cause and effect. In this case the cause is advances in technology and medical science, and the effect or result is the decline in infant mortality rates.

Since "owing to" is a phrase linker, the grammatical subject of the original sentence (there) and the verb (have been) are removed when creating the new sentence.

**Answer (b):**

b) Since there have been advances in technology and medical science, infant mortality rates have declined substantially in recent years.

"Since" is a subordinator, so you can combine the sentences without making any changes.

Remember to use the comma between the two parts of the sentence because the clauses have been inverted.

**Exercise 9:**

It was the most expensive restaurant in town.

It had rude staff and provided the worst service.

**Answer (a):**

a) It was the most expensive restaurant in town, besides having rude staff and providing the worst service.

"Besides" is a phrase linker, so use the present participle form of both verbs in the second original sentence. Accordingly, "had" becomes "having" and "provide" becomes "providing."

**Answer (b):**

There are two possible answers.

b) In addition to being the most expensive restaurant in town, it had rude staff and provided the worst service.

b) In addition to having rude staff and providing the worst service, it was the most expensive restaurant in town.

"In addition to" is a phrase linker, so the present participle forms are used in the phrase containing this word.

The order of the original sentences can be changed since there is no cause and effect relationship between these ideas.

**Exercise 10:**

*Now try to combine these three sentences:*

The judge did not punish the criminal justly.

He decided to grant a lenient sentence.

He did not send out a message to deter potential offenders in the future.

**Answer (a):**

a) Instead of punishing the criminal justly and thereby sending out a message to deter potential offenders in the future, the judge decided to grant a lenient sentence.

**Answer (b):**

b) Rather than punishing the criminal justly in order to send out a message to deter potential offenders in the future, the judge decided to grant a lenient sentence.

As you will see, answers A and B are somewhat similar in their construction.

"Instead of" and "rather than" need to be used with the present particle form (punishing).

"Thereby" must be followed by the present participle form (sending).

However, "in order to" needs to take the base form of the verb (send).

The base form is the verb before any change has been made to it, like making the –ed or –ing forms. The following are examples of base forms of verbs: eat, sleep, work, play.

## Using Correct Grammar and Punctuation

Mechanical conventions are the rules of grammar and punctuation that are necessary in order to write accurately and correctly.

This section is intended as a basic overview of some of the most important mechanical conventions.

## Comparatives and Superlatives – Avoid Using Double Forms:

Use the comparative form when comparing two things.

The comparative form consists of the adjective plus –er when the adjective has two syllables or less.

pretty → prettier

*Avoid making a double comparative:*

INCORRECT: more prettier

When the adjective has more than two syllables, the adjective should be preceded by the word "more" in order to form the comparative.

beautiful → more beautiful

Examples:

Tom is taller than his brother.

Tom is more intelligent than his brother.

If you are comparing more than two things, you must use the superlative form.

As a general rule, the superlative form consists of the adjective plus –est when the adjective has two syllables or less.

pretty → prettiest

*Avoid making a double superlative:*

INCORRECT: most prettiest

To form the superlative for adjectives that have more than two syllables, the adjective should be preceded by the word "most".

beautiful → most beautiful

<u>Examples:</u>

Tom is the tallest boy in his class.

Tom is the most intelligent boy in his class.

**Correct Use of *Its* and *It's*:**

"Its" is a possessive pronoun, while "it's" is a contraction of "it is."

CORRECT: It's high time you started to study.

INCORRECT: Its high time you started to study.

The sentence could also be stated as follows: It is high time that you started to study.

Since the contracted form of "it is" is used in the alternative sentence, "it's" is the correct form.

CORRECT: A snake sheds its skin at least once a year.

INCORRECT: A snake sheds it's skin at least once a year.

"Its" is a possessive pronoun referring to the snake, so the apostrophe should not be used.

**Correct Use of *Their*, *There*, and *They're*:**

"Their" is a plural possessive pronoun.

"There" is used to describe the location of something.

"They're" is a contraction of "they are."

CORRECT: Their house is made of brick and concrete.

INCORRECT: There house is made of brick and concrete.

INCORRECT: They're house is made of brick and concrete.

In this case, "their" is the possessive pronoun explaining to whom the house belongs.

CORRECT: He attended college with his cousins living there in California.

INCORRECT: He attended college with his cousins living their in California.

INCORRECT: He attended college with his cousins living they're in California.

"There" is referring to the state of California in the example above, so it is used to talk about the location.

CORRECT: They're away on vacation at the moment.

INCORRECT: Their away on vacation at the moment.

INCORRECT: There away on vacation at the moment.

The sentence could also be written as follows: They are away on vacation at the moment.

"They're" is a contraction of "they are," so the apostrophe needs to be used.

**Correct Use of *Were*, *Where*, and *We're*:**

"Were" is the past tense of the verb "are."

"Where" is used to inquire about or describe the location of something.

"We're" is a contraction of "we are."

CORRECT: They were going to call you, but the phone was out of order.

INCORRECT: They where going to call you, but the phone was out of order.

INCORRECT: They we're going to call you, but the phone was out of order.

"Were" is the past form of the verb in the sentence above.

CORRECT: Where is the mall located?

INCORRECT: Were is the mall located?

INCORRECT: We're is the mall located?

"Where" needs to be used because the sentence is making an inquiry about the location of the mall.

CORRECT: We're so happy that you got accepted into college.

INCORRECT: Were so happy that you got accepted into college.

INCORRECT: Where so happy that you got accepted into college.

The sentence could be written as follows: We are so happy that you got accepted into college.

"We're" is a contraction of "we are," so the apostrophe needs to be used.

*Avoid the "is where" construction:*

CORRECT: An identity crisis, which is the experience of confusion about one's life goals and ambitions, often occurs in middle age.

INCORRECT: An identity crisis is where there is the experience of confusion about one's life goals and ambitions, and it often occurs in middle age.

The construction in the second sentence may be used in informal speaking, but such constructions should be avoided in your essay.

## Misplaced Modifiers:

Modifiers are phrases that describe other parts of a sentence. The modifier should always be placed directly before or after the noun to which it relates.

Now look at these examples:

CORRECT: Like Minnesota, Wisconsin gets extremely cold in the winter.

INCORRECT: Like Minnesota, it gets extremely cold in Wisconsin in the winter.

The phrase "like Minnesota" is an adjectival phrase that modifies the noun "Wisconsin."

Therefore, "Wisconsin" must come directly after the comma.

Here are two more examples:

CORRECT: While at the mall, a gang of youths committed a robbery.

INCORRECT: While at the mall, a robbery was committed.

The adverbial phrase "while at the mall" modifies the noun phrase "a gang of youths," so this noun phrase needs to come after the adverbial phrase.

## Parallelism:

When giving items in a series, be sure to use consistent forms.

CORRECT: The position involves answering phone calls, writing letters, and getting supplies.

INCORRECT: The position involves answering phone calls, writing letters, and get supplies.

All of the items in the series should be in the –ing form.

CORRECT: I saw Tom's accident yesterday, and I tried to help.

INCORRECT: I saw Tom's accident yesterday, and I try to help.

Both parts of the sentence are describing actions that occurred yesterday, so the past tense (ending in –ed) needs to be used for both verbs.

## Punctuation and Independent Clauses – Avoiding Run-On Sentences:

Run-on sentences are those that use commas to join independent clauses together, instead of correctly using the period.

An independent clause contains a grammatical subject and verb. It therefore can stand alone as its own sentence.

The first word of the independent clause should begin with a capital letter, and the clause should be preceded by a period.

CORRECT: I thought I would live in this city forever. Then I lost my job.

INCORRECT: I thought I would live in this city forever, then I lost my job.

"Then I lost my job" is a complete sentence. It has a grammatical subject (I) and a verb (lost). The independent clause must be preceded by a period, and the first word of the new sentence must begin with a capital letter.

Alternatively, an appropriate conjunction can be used to join the independent clauses:

I thought I would live in this city forever, and then I lost my job.

## Punctuation and Quotation Marks:

Punctuation should be enclosed within the final quotation mark when giving dialogue.

CORRECT: "I can't believe you bought a new car," Sam remarked.

INCORRECT: "I can't believe you bought a new car", Sam remarked.

In the example below, the word "exclaimed" shows that the exclamation point is needed.

CORRECT: "I can't believe you bought a new car!" Sam exclaimed.

INCORRECT: "I can't believe you bought a new car"! Sam exclaimed.

However, if the quotation is stated indirectly, no quotation marks should be used.

CORRECT: Sam exclaimed that he couldn't believe that I had bought a new car.

INCORRECT: Sam exclaimed that "he couldn't believe that I had bought a new car."

## Punctuation for Items in a Series:

When using "and" and "or" for more than two items in a series, be sure to use the comma before the words "and" and "or."

CORRECT: You need to bring a tent, sleeping bag, and flashlight.

INCORRECT: You need to bring a tent, sleeping bag and flashlight.

Notice the use of the comma after the word "bag" and before the word "and" in the series.

CORRECT: Students can call, write a letter, or send an email.

INCORRECT: Students can call, write a letter or send an email.

Notice the use of the comma after the word "letter" and before the word "or" in the series.

## Restrictive and Non-restrictive Modifiers:

Restrictive modifiers are clauses or phrases that provide essential information in order to identify the grammatical subject. Restrictive modifiers should not be preceded by a comma.

Example: My sister who lives in Indianapolis is a good swimmer.

In this case, the speaker has more than one sister, and she is identifying which sister she is talking about by giving the essential information "who lives in Indianapolis."

On the other hand, a non-restrictive modifier is a clause or phrase that provides extra information about a grammatical subject in a sentence. A non-restrictive modifier must be preceded by a comma.

Non-restrictive modifiers are also known as non-essential modifiers.

Example: My sister, who lives in Indianapolis, is a good swimmer.

In this case, the speaker has only one sister. Therefore, the information about her sister's city of residence is not essential in order to identify which sister she is talking about.

The words "who lives in Indianapolis" form a non-restrictive modifier.

## Sentence Fragments:

A sentence fragment is a group of words that does not express a complete train of thought.

CORRECT: I like Denver because it has a great university.

INCORRECT: I like Denver. Because it has a great university.

In the second example, "because it has a great university" is not a complete thought. This idea needs to be joined with the previous clause in order to be grammatically correct.

## Subject-Verb Agreement:

Subjects must agree with verbs in number.

Subject-verb agreement can be confusing when there are intervening words in a sentence.

CORRECT: The flowers in the pots in the garden grow quickly.

INCORRECT: The flowers in the pots in the garden grows quickly.

The grammatical subject in the above sentence is "flowers," not "garden," so the plural form of the verb (*grow*) needs to be used.

CORRECT: Each person in the groups of students needs to pay attention to the instructions.

INCORRECT: Each person in the groups of students need to pay attention to the instructions.

The grammatical subject in the above sentence is "each person," not "students." "Each" is singular and therefore needs the singular form of the verb (*needs*).

**Using Correct Grammar and Punctuation – Exercises**

*Each of the sentences below has problems with grammar and punctuation. Find the errors in the sentences and correct them. You may wish to refer to the advice in the previous section as you do the exercise.*

*The answers are provided on the page following the exercises.*

1) I haven't seen her or her sister. Since they went away to college.

2) People who like to get up early in the morning in order to drink more coffee is likely to become easily tired in the afternoon.

3) Were we're you when we called you yesterday?

4) She is the most happiest person that I know.

5) Hanging from the knob on the bedroom door, Tom thought the new shirt was his favorite.

6) I ran across the street to speak to her, then she surprised me by saying "that she had bought a new car."

7) Its common for a magazine to have better sales if it mentions computers, handhelds or other new technology on it's cover.

8) After losing long-term employment, many people suffer from anxiety, loneliness and get depressed.

9) Each student in the class who will take the series of exams on advanced mathematics need to study in advance.

10) Their are several reasons why there having problems with they're children.

**Using Correct Grammar and Punctuation – Answers**

1) I haven't seen her or her sister since they went away to college.

2) People who like to get up early in the morning in order to drink more coffee are likely to become easily tired in the afternoon.

3) Where were you when we called you yesterday?

4) She is the happiest person that I know.

5) Hanging from the knob on the bedroom door, the new shirt was Tom's favorite.

6) I ran across the street to speak to her. Then she surprised me by saying that she had bought a new car.

7) It's common for a magazine to have better sales if it mentions computers, handhelds, or other new technology on its cover.

8) After losing long-term employment, many people suffer from anxiety, loneliness, and depression.

9) Each student in the class who will take the series of exams on advanced mathematics needs to study in advance.

10) There are several reasons why they're having problems with their children.

**Sample Essays:**

*Look at each essay below. Then identify the thesis statement in each one. Note how each paragraph in the main body gives and elaborating idea and expands upon it. Also study the structure of the introduction and conclusion, as well as the overall structure of each essay itself. Finally, you may wish to make a note of the high-level academic vocabulary used in the essays.*

**Essay Question 1** – Is it ever socially acceptable to be pleased when others suffer?

While feeling pleasure when others suffer is a human emotion to which most of us would not be so quick to admit, there are occasions when it is socially acceptable to take pleasure in the pain of others. Consider, for example, the gratification that the people of European countries would have experienced when Hitler was defeated during the Second World War. Punishment for crime is another occasion where it is not considered untoward to experience satisfaction over the suffering of others. That is to say, although being pleased to see others stricken is normally not acceptable in a civilized society, there are exceptions to this general rule when others have broken the society's norms during times of war or when a criminal is to be punished for his or her wrongdoing.

Unfortunately, in modern times we have all too often seen dictators or other despotic rulers who treat the members of their societies harshly, and in such situations, the reactions of those subjected to these regimes is certainly socially justifiable. Adolph Hitler, arguably the most notorious dictator of the twentieth century, committed countless heinous acts against the inhabitants of several European countries during World War II. Due to his atrocities, previously contented residents of many towns and villages had to flee their homes in fear, leaving behind all of their worldly possessions. The most unfortunate of these persecuted individuals were submitted to unthinkable states of existence in the many death camps that Hitler oversaw. Because they were forced to live in such unimaginable conditions, those that Hitler persecuted must have been gratified when the dictator faced adversity during the war. Once Hitler had encountered the final ultimatum of surrender or death and his regime was overthrown, the relief and satisfaction openly expressed around the world on a personal level was immense.

The notion that the punishment should fit the crime is another instance of the acceptability of taking pleasure in another's suffering. Criminal law, which has been created according to traditional social convention, has been established to ensure that offenders will be justly tried and punished for their crimes. When someone has broken the norms of society in this way, other members of the community feel satisfied because they believe that justice has been served when the offender has been punished. In addition, punishing social wrongs can act as a deterrent to would-be criminals, thereby further reinforcing social norms.

Whereas taking delight in the misfortune of others is a trait that normally would not receive social approbation, the circumstances faced in war and crime fall outside this conventional social restriction. However, it is doubtful that *schadenfreude* will ever be considered a socially desirable quality outside these two situations.

**Essay Question 2** – Most Americans have access to computers and cell phones on a daily basis, making email and text messaging extremely popular. While some people argue that email and texting are now the most convenient forms of personal communication, others believe that electronic communication technology is often used inappropriately. Write an essay for an audience of educated adults in which you take a position on this topic. Be sure to provide reasons and examples to support your viewpoint.

**Sample Essay 2:**

There is no disputing the fact that email and SMS technologies have made our lives easier in a variety of ways. Nevertheless, many of us will have had the experience of falling out with a friend or loved one over an email or text message whose content was poorly written or misconstrued. Clearly, there are certain drawbacks to emails and texts since electronic messaging cannot capture the nuances and subtleties of verbal communication. Modern forms of communication such as electronic mail and SMS messaging can cause problems with personal relationships because of three main shortcomings with these media: their impersonal nature, their inability to capture tone and sarcasm, and their easy accessibility at times of anger.

Depending upon the context, the recipient of an email or text message may consider this mode of communication to be insensitive or uncaring. Although email may be practical for conveying straightforward information or facts, electronic messaging would be remarkably inappropriate for events like announcing a death. There is no direct human contact in emails and texts, and during times of loss or tragedy, human warmth and depth of emotion can only truly be conveyed through a phone call, or better still, by talking face to face.

A further problem with emails and texts is that they do not always accurately express the tone which the writer has intended. For instance, it might be possible for the recipient of a sarcastic email message to take its contents literally. The tone of the message may seem abundantly clear to the person who sent it, but sarcastic or ironically humorous utterances can only really be communicated in speech through the tone and inflection of the voice. Without the aid of tone and inflection, certain phrases in an email may come across as demanding, indifferent, or rude.

The danger of having an accessible messaging service readily at hand during times of high emotion is another insidious problem with electronic media. In this day and age, we have heard stories not only of personal break ups that have been conducted by text, but also of employers who fire their staff by email message. Unless the writer of the message has the discipline and self-control to give him or herself a period of reasoned contemplation before sending the communication, he or she might send a regrettable message that can cause irretrievable damage to a relationship.

While email and texts may therefore be useful for certain aspects of our daily lives, these communication methods need to be handled with care in some situations, particularly when they could be seen as insensitive, when it is possible that the recipient might misinterpret the meaning, or when composed at times of personal agitation or stress. The writer of the message should use judgment and common sense in order to avoid the ill feelings that may be caused to the recipient in these cases.

Made in the USA
San Bernardino, CA
12 April 2014